THE WHITE PROBLEM IN AMERICA

The
WHITE
Problem
in America

By the Editors of Ebony

Johnson Publishing Company, Inc.

Chicago 1966

Publisher's Statement

In the entire history of the period during which the area of the North American Continent now known as the United States has been occupied by white Europeans and their descendants, the white man has been trying to explain away the Negro.

From the landing of the first Negroes at Jamestown, Va., in 1619 to the Emancipation Proclamation in 1863 the explanation was, "They are better off as slaves here than they were as tribesmen in the African jungle." When the Christian conscience could no longer deny that it was sin to treat a human as a chattel (and the ecomomy of the South could no longer truly support a slave society), Negroes, ostensibly, were given their freedom and awarded the honorary degree of humanity. But, despite the 13th, 14th and 15th Amendments to the Constitution and despite the fact that once having been given citizenship, he automatically fell under the protection of the Constitution with all the guardianship supposedly implicit in the Bill of Rights, the Negro found that his "honorary" degree of humanity had no real meaning.

He was explained away again for nearly 100 years as "not being ready yet." He was "protected" by the courts which legally said, "You shall be kept separate, though equal. You are a second class citizen."

Then came World War II, the Communist conspiracy, the black nations' fight for freedom from colonialism and a reexamination of the Christian faith which brought forth the idea that skin color was not a true measure of a man's humanity. Finally, in 1954, the U.S. Supreme Court ruled that the doctrine of separate but equal was untenable under the Constitution.

Today, the explaining away is a little more difficult. Enough Negroes have proved that, given an equal chance, they can measure up to the best. Now the explaining away takes the form of, "Things are better today than they were yesterday and will be better tomorrow than they are today. Have patience. Don't demonstrate. Everything will come about in due time."

But the time is now and the Negro in the pulpits, in the streets, in the schools, at the polls, in the halls of justice and in the legislative bodies of the land has emphasized that today he has earned his humanity and his full rights as a citizen.

What has held him up?

The unthinking white man—Mr. Charlie, Whitey, The Man—the unthinking white man who is the symbol to Negroes of all those whites who have "stood in the doorways" to keep the Negro back.

This brings us to this special issue, "The White Problem in America," and its reason for being.

For more than a decade through books, magazines, newspapers, TV and radio, the white man has been trying to solve the race problem through studying the Negro. We feel that the answer lies in a more thorough study of the man who created the problem. In this issue we, as Negroes, look at the white man today with the hope that our effort will tempt him to look at himself more thoroughly. With a better understanding of himself, we trust that he may then understand us better—and this nation's most vital problem can then be solved.

John H. Johnson

Editor's Preface

A special issue like the August 1965 *Ebony* is not something that just happens. It takes a great deal of thought, a great deal of planning and then many extra hours of just plain hard work by everyone in the Johnson Publishing Company— circulation and promotion staffs as well as the editorial people —to bring it off.

Most of the editorial staffers in addition to doing their normal work of editing pieces sent in by contributors undertook the writing of at least one major article each. You will find their bylines on these pieces. Other staffers, particularly Assistant Editor Robert Hunter and *Jet* staffer Art Sears, worked over and beyond the call of duty to help make this issue a success.

A particular vote of thanks goes to JPC artists Norman Hunter, Herbert Temple, Cecil Ferguson and Thomas Greene for a yeoman job performed in the art department. Editorial secretary Beverly Adams expedited all special issue correspondence and the library staff under Mrs. Lucille Phinnie gave the issue special priority in all research.

We offer a special vote of thanks to our outside contributors—Whitney Young, Carl Rowan, Louis Lomax, Dr. Martin Luther King Jr., John Killens and James Baldwin—for the dispatch with which they completed their tasks. The ever-busy Baldwin first received his assignment in Vienna, started the writing of it in Paris and completed it in Zurich, Switzerland, as Paris Editor Charles L. Sanders stood by waiting to cable the manuscript to Chicago so that we would have it by press time.

It was a hectic, hard, nerve-wracking period but, finally, it was done. We celebrated with several bottles of champagne when the first advance copies arrived from the printer and then began the nervous wait for reader reaction once the magazine went on sale.

The reaction was quick and, to our great delight, positive. Letters poured in from subscribers who said that they had bought extra copies to distribute to friends. Big city newspapers and national magazines carried stories about the issue. College professors used it in classes. Ministers preached from it in their pulpits. And many whites who had never seen the magazine before bought it, read it, and searched their souls.

The sales climbed far above those of anything we had published and, strangely, the issue is still selling although it has already gone above a million. We had felt from the beginning that "The White Problem in America" would be a significant milestone in our progress. It has more than lived up to our expectations.

Herbert Nipson
Managing Editor

Contents

LERONE BENNETT JR.

The White Problem in America

There is no Negro problem in America.

The problem of race in America, insofar as that problem is related to packets of melanin in men's skins, is a white problem. And in order to solve that problem we must seek its source, not in the Negro but in the white American (in the process by which he was educated, in the needs and complexes he expresses through racism) and in the structure of the white community (in the power arrangements and the illicit uses of racism in the scramble for scarce values: power, prestige, income).

The depth and intensity of the race problem in America is, in part, a result of a 100-year flight from that unpalatable truth. It was a stroke of genius really for white Americans to give Negro Americans the name of their problem, thereby focusing attention on symptoms (the Negro and the Negro community) instead of causes (the white man and the white community).

When we say that the causes of the race problem are rooted in the white American and the white community, we mean that the power is the white American's and so is the responsibility. We mean that the white American created, *invented* the race problem and that his fears and frailties are responsible for the urgency of the problem.

When we say that the fears of white Americans are at the root of the problem, we mean that the white American is a problem to himself and that because he is a problem to himself he has made others problems to themselves.

When we say that the white American is a problem to himself, we mean that racism is a reflection of personal and collective anxieties lodged deep in the hearts and minds of white Americans.

By all this, we must understand that Harlem is a white-made thing and that in order to understand Harlem we must go not to Harlem but to the conscience of white Americans and we must ask not what is Harlem but what have you made of Harlem. Why did you create it? And why do you need it?

The validity of this approach has been underlined by many experts, including Gunnar Myrdal, who began his massive work on the Negro (*An American Dilemma*) by admitting, in so many words, that he had studied the wrong people. "Although the Negro problem is a moral issue both to Negroes and to whites in America," he wrote, "we shall in this book have to give *primary* attention to what goes on in the minds of white Americans. . . . When the present investigator started his inquiry, his preconception was that it had to be focused on the Negro people and their peculiarities. . . . But as he proceeded in his studies into the Negro problem, it became increasingly evident that little, if anything, could be scientifically explained in terms of the peculiarities of the Negroes themselves. . . . It is thus the white majority group that naturally determines the Negro's 'place.' All our attempts to reach scientific explanations of why the Negroes are what they are and why they live as they do have regularly led to determinants on the white side of the racial line. In the practical and political struggles of affecting changes, the views and attitudes of the white Americans are likewise strategic. The Negro's entire life, and, consequently, also his opinions on the Negro problem, are, in the main, to be considered as secondary reactions to more primary pressures from the side of the dominant white majority."

Scores of investigators have reached the same conclusions: namely, that the peculiarities of white folk are the primary determinants of the American social problem.

Consider, for example, the testimony of James Weldon Johnson, the great Negro leader:

". . . the main difficulty of the race question does not lie so much in the actual condition of the blacks as it does in the mental attitude of the whites."

Johnson also said:

"The race question involves the saving of black America's body and white America's soul."

White Americans have perceived the same truth. Author Ray Stannard Baker wrote:

"It keeps coming to me that this is more a white man's problem than it is a Negro problem."

So it seemed also to Thomas P. Bailey, a Southern white.

"The real problem," he wrote, "is not the Negro but the white man's attitude toward the Negro."

And again:

"Yes, we Southerners need a freedom from suspicion, fear, anxiety, doubt, unrest, hate, contempt, disgust, and all the rest of the race-feeling-begotten brood of vituperation."

Ralph McGill, another Southerner, made a similar observation.

"We do not have a minority problem," he said, "but a majority problem."

Of like tone and tenor was the perceptive statement of Thomas Merton, the Trappist monk.

"The purpose of non-violent protest, in its deepest and most spiritual dimension is then to awaken the conscience of the white man to the awful responsibility of his injustice and sin, so that he will be able to see that the Negro problem is really a *White* problem: that the cancer of injustice and hate which is eating white society and is only partly manifested in racial segregation with its consequences, *is rooted in the heart of the white man himself.* [Merton's emphasis.]

It is there, "in the heart of the white man himself," in his peculiarities, in his mental attitudes, in his need for "a freedom from suspicion, fear, anxiety, doubt, unrest, hate, contempt, disgust," that we must situate the racial problem. For here, as elsewhere, the proper statement of the problem, though not a solution, is at least a strong step in the right direction. For too long now, we have focused attention on the Negro, forgetting that the Negro is who he is because white people are what they are. In our innocence—and in our guile—we have spoken of Negro crime, when the problem is white crime; we have spoken of the need for educating Negroes, when the problem is the education of whites; we have spoken of the lack of responsible Negro leadership, when the problem is the lack of responsible white leadership.

The premise of this special issue is that America can no longer afford the luxury of ignoring its real problem: the white problem. To be sure, Negroes are not blameless. It takes two to tango and the Negro, at the very least, is responsible for accepting the grapes of degradation. But that, you see, has nothing to do with the man who is responsible for the degradation. The prisoner is always free to try to escape. What the jailer must decide is whether he will help escaping prisoners over the wall or shoot them in the back. And the lesson of American life is that no Negro—no matter how much money he accumulated, no matter how many degrees he earned—has ever crossed completely the wall of color-caste, except by adopting the expedient of passing. Let us come to that point and stand on it: Negroes are condemned in America, not because they are poor, not because they are uneducated, not because they are brown or black—Negroes are condemned in America because they are Negroes, i.e., because of an idea of the Negro and of the Negro's place in the white American's mind.

When we say that the race problem in America is a white problem, we mean that the real problem is an irrational and antiscientific idea of race in the minds of white Americans. Let us not be put off by recitations of "social facts." Social facts do not make Negroes; on the contrary, it is the idea of the Negro which organizes and distorts social facts in order to make "Negroes." Hitler, who had some experience in the matter, said social facts are sustainers and not creators of prejudice. In other words: If we assume that Negroes are inferior and if we use that assumption as a rationale for giving Negroes poor schools, poor jobs, and poor housing, we will sooner or later create a condition which "confirms" our assumption and "justifies" additional discrimination.

No: social facts are not at the heart of the problem. In fact, social facts tell us more about whites, about their needs, insecurities, and immaturities, than about Negroes. Many Negroes are poor, but so are forty to fifty million American whites. Some Negro women have babies out of wedlock, but so do millions of middle-class American white women. Racists and millions of "normal" white Americans know this; but they are not and cannot be convinced *for their knowledge precedes facts*. Because the *idea of race* intervenes between the concrete Negro and the social fact, Negro intellectuals and white racists rarely, if ever, understand each other. What the white racist means by social facts is that there are "Negro social facts," that Negroes, by virtue of their birth, have within them a magical substance that gives facts a certain quality. He means by that that there is a Negro and a white way of being poor, that there is a Negro and white way of being immoral, that, in his mind, white people and black people are criminals in different ways. As a result of this magical thinking, millions on millions of white Americans are unable to understand that slums, family disorganization and illiteracy are not the causes of the racial problem, but the end product of the problem.

That problem, in essence, is racism. But we misunderstand racism completely if we do not understand that racism is a mask for a much deeper problem involving not the victims of racism but the perpetrators. We must come to see that racism in America is the poor man's way out and the powerful man's way in: *a way in* for the powerful who derive enormous profits from the divisions in our society; *a way out* for the frustrated and frightened who excuse economic, social, and sexual failure by convincing themselves that no matter how low they fall they are still higher and better than Harry Belafonte, Ralphe Bunche, Cassius Clay and Martin Luther King Jr., all rolled up into one.

We must realize also that prejudice on all levels reflects a high level of personal and social disorganization in the white community. On a personal level, particularly among lower-income and middle-income whites, prejudice is an avenue of flight, a cry for help from desperate men stifling in the prisons of their skins. Growing up in a culture permeated with prejudice, imbibing it, so to speak, with their milk, millions of white Americans find that Negroes are useful screens to hide themselves from themselves. Repeated studies have shown that Negro hate is, in part, a socially-sanctioned outlet for personal and social anxieties and frustrations. From this stand-point, racism is a flight from the self, a flight from freedom, a flight from the intolerable burdens of being a man in a menacing world.

Not all white Americans are biased, of course, but all white Americans and all Americans have been affected by bias. This issue suggests that we need to know a great deal more about how white Americans exist with their whiteness, and how some white Americans, to a certain extent, rise above early conditioning through non-Communist radicalism or liberalism.

The racist impulse, which white Americans express in different ways but which almost all do express, either by rebelling against it or by accepting it, reflects deep forces in the dominant community. There is considerable evidence, for example, that the culture's stress on success and status induces exaggerated anxieties and fears which are displaced onto the area of race relations. The fear of failure, the fear of competitors, the fear of losing status, of not living in the "right" neighborhood, of not having the "right" friends or the "right" gadgets: these fears weigh heavily on the minds of millions of white Americans and lead to a search for avenues of escape. And so the second- or third-generation factory worker or the poor white farmer who finds himself at a dead end with a nagging wife, a problem child, and a past-due bill may take out his aggressive feelings and his frustrations in race hatred.

The concept of the Negro problem as a white problem suggests that there is a need for additional research to determine to what extent Negro hate is a defense against self-hate. It also suggests that attention should be directed to the power gains of highly-placed politicians and businessmen who derive direct power gains from the division of our population into mutually hostile groups. By using racism, consciously or unconsciously, to divert public discontent and to boost the shaky egos of white groups on or near the bottom, men of power in America have played a key role in making racism a permanent structure of our society.

It is fashionable nowadays to think of racism as a vast

impersonal system for which no one is responsible. But this is still another evasion. Racism did not fall from the sky; it was not secreted by insects. No: racism in America was made by men, neighborhood by neighborhood, law by law, restrictive covenant by restrictive covenant, deed by deed.

It is not remembered often enough today that the color-caste vise, which constricts both Negroes and whites, was created by men of power who artificially separated Negroes and whites who got on famously in Colonial America. This is a fact of capital importance in considering the white problem. The first black immigrants in America were not slaves; nor, for the most part, were the first white immigrants free. Most of the English colonists, in the beginning, were white indentured servants possessing remarkably little racial prejudice.

Back there, in the beginning, Negro and white indentured servants worked together in the same fields, lived together in the same huts and played together after working hours. And, of course, they also mated and married. So widespread was intermingling during this period that Peter Fontaine and other writers said the land "swarmed with mulatto" children.

From 1619 to about 1660, a period of primary importance in the history of America, America was not ruled by color. Some, perhaps all, of the first group of African-Americans worked out their terms of servitude and were freed. Within a few years. Negroes were accumulating property, pounds, and indentured servants. One Negro immigrant, Richard Johnson, even imported a white man and held him in servitude.

The breaking of the developing bonds of community between Negro and white Americans began with a conscious decision by the power structures of Colonial America. In the 1660s, men of power in the colonies decided that human slavery, based on skin color, was to be the linchpin of the new society. Having made this decision, they were forced to take another, more ominous step. Nature does not prepare men for the roles of master or racist. It requires rigid training, long persisted in, to make men and women deny other men and women and themselves. Men must be carefully taught to hate, and the lessons learned by one generation must be relearned by the next.

The Negro and white working class of the 1660s, the bulk of the population, had not been prepared for the roles outlined in the new script of statutes. It was necessary, therefore, to teach them that they could not deal with each other as fellow human beings.

How was this done?

It was done by an assault on the Negro's body and the white man's soul.

Legislatures ground out laws of every imaginable description and vigilantes whipped the doubtful into line. Behind the nightriders, of course, stood God himself in the person of parsons who blessed the rupture in human relations with words from the Bible.

Who was responsible for this policy?

The planters, the aristocrats, the parsons, the lawyers, the Founding Fathers—*the good people:* they created the white problem.

Men would say later that there is a natural antipathy between Negro and white Americans. But the record belies them. Negro and white Americans were taught to hate and fear each other by words, sermons, whips, and signed papers. The process continued over a period of more than 100 years, a period which saw the destruction of the Negro family and the exclusion of Negro workers from one skilled trade after another. Nor did white men escape. They saw, dimly, what they were doing to themselves and to others and they drew back from themselves, afraid. But they did not stop; perhaps they could not stop. For, by now, racism had become central to their needs and to their identity. Moreover, they were moved by dark and turbulent forces within. The evidence of their deeds bred fear and guilt which, in turn, led to more anxiety and guilt and additional demands for exclusion and aggression. Propelled by this dynamic, the whole process of excluding and fearing reached something of a peak in the first decade of the Twentieth Century with a carnival of Jim Crow in the South and a genteel movement which blanketed the North with restrictive covenants. The net result was a system of color-caste which divided communities, North and South, into mutually hostile groups.

Since that time, investigators have focused almost all of their attention on the Negro community, with the resulting neglect of primary determinants on the white side of the racial line. By asserting that the Negro problem is predominantly a white problem, this issue summons us to a new beginning and suggests that anything that hides the white American from a confrontation with himself and with the fact that he must change before the Negro can change is a major part of the problem.

JOHN N. WOODFORD

White Hate Groups

Minutes after the news of the Dallas assassination of President John F. Kennedy circled the globe, the nation was paralyzed between grief and fear. As whispers became murmurs, murmurs became rumors and rumors became opinion, a devastating indictment burst upon the world: "The radical right is taking over! The hate groups did it!"

The charge proved false. But was the suspicion justifiable? Who basked in the climate of hatred which encouraged the slaying? Whose children cheered the President's death in their classrooms? Who made liberalism, democracy, integration and world peace—sturdy planks of the Kennedy platform—detestable to millions of white Americans? Who has preyed upon confused whites and banded them into a spectrum of hate groups which threaten not only Negroes and other minorities, but also their liberal and moderate white compatriots? The answer: leaders of the fanatical right.

Rich and cunning, radical right leaders use the mass media to expose their feverish message to millions and millions of Americans every day. They vary their bait depending upon the social and economic status of those they wish to hook. In some areas they are rabidly anti-Negro, anti-Jew and anti-

Catholic; in other areas, they lace their brew with anti-Communism or pretend to be protecting individual liberties. Some are hooded, others are hoodwinkers who, like matadors, wave the flag in one hand and stab the Constitution with the other. Although they are not yet united, the white hate groups are interconnected, and their alarming propaganda is essentially the same. The Ku Klux Klan, the White Citizens' Councils, the John Birch Society, the Minutemen, and the American Nazi Party—plus the multitude of fringe and front groups—all hate the same ideas, people and institutions in the world today.

There is, however, variety in their unity. The Klan's poor whites are jealously protecting the kitchen scraps of the Southern economy. These pickings are the leftovers of the more educated but hardly more moral middle-class whites who formed the White Citizens Councils. The Councils, in turn, collaborate with Northern rightist groups like the Birch Society, which gives vulgar racism a face-lifting job with the cosmetic of "anti-Communism." Most right wing groups reap profits and power from the fantasy of a massive Communist conspiracy in America. Others, like the Minutemen, simply believe the simple horror story and practice guerrilla warfare in rigid secrecy. And the whole body of the radical right is completed by self-proclaimed Fascist groups like the American Nazis, whose foul-mouthed propaganda makes them another handy scapegoat for the more crafty white hate groups. By denouncing the Nazis and Klan the more sober hate groups hope to conceal the connections between themselves and the discredited hatemongers.

But the "Klounsel" of the Ku Klux Klan, Matt Murphy, crudely identified the chief targets of all the white hate groups in his defense of civil rights worker Viola Liuzzo's accused murderer: "I thought I'd never see the day when Communists and niggers and white niggers and Jews were flying under the banner of the United Nations flag, not the American flag we fought for . . . Do you know those big black niggers were driven by the woman . . . one white woman and these niggers . . . riding through your country. Communists dominate them niggers!"

Once he was freed, Collie Leroy Wilkins, the accused killer, was cheered by the Klan as an even greater hero than Sheriff Lawrence Rainey and Deputy Cecil Price, Byron De La Beckwith and Lester Maddox.

Now the whipping boy of the other radical rightists, the Klan was once run by Southern planters and politicians who called themselves Dragons, Furies, Goblins and Night Hawks. At the bottom of this ranking were the poor whites, called Ghouls. Formed in 1865 in Pulaski, Tenn., the Klan has never been the chivalrous and just organization of Southern legend. Robed to scare the Negroes who believed in ghosts, the Klan's first goal was to frighten Negroes out of exercising their political freedom. Soon, however, the Ghouls became uncontrollable. They indulged in rape, lust, sadism and murder until, disgusted by the bloodshed, the more intelligent whites quit the Klan.

The Klan faded, but after World War I, a Methodist minister who had been expelled from his pulpit reorganized the dregs of Southern society and formalized brutality into religious rites. Unlike the first Klan, this one was not specifically formed to terrorize Negroes. But the result was the same. In Moultrie, Ga., in 1921, a *Washington Eagle* reporter witnessed one of some 5,000 Negro lynchings in this country since 1859: "The Negro was unsexed and made to eat a portion of his anatomy. . . . Castrated and in indescribable torture, the Negro asked for a cigarette, lit it and blew the smoke in the face of his tormentors. The pyre was lit and a hundred men and women, old and young, grandmothers among them, joined and danced while the Negro burned."

Claiming to fight communism, which it saw in Jews, Negroes and Catholics, this second Klan faded in the 1940s. The third and current Klan combines the former two. It seeks to deprive the Negro of his civil liberties and is suspected of committing recent murders of civil rights workers, of the Birmingham Sunday school girls and Lt. Col. Lemuel Penn. But this Klan mimics its more "respectable" cousins on the right by charging that the civil rights movement is Communistic.

The Klan's most kissing cousin is the White Citizens Council. Founded in Indianola, Miss., to fight the 1954 Supreme Court decision outlawing school segregation, the Council wooed middle class Southerners, says a Council leader, "through the service clubs . . . Rotary or Kiwanis or Civitans or Exchange or Lions." But even Council spokesmen were forced to admit that their hate propaganda included not only Klan-ish diatribes but also Nazi pamphlets. Defending this hate literature, a Councilman said: "Some of these groups are anti-Semitic; however, all of the religious groups—including all Protestant, Catholic and Jewish—have been pushing the anti-segregation issue and it is time for all of us to speak out for separation of the black and white races, regardless of our race and creed."

The Councils strive to crush their opposition, black and white, economically rather than physically, but they are unable to hide their bond with the Klan. When the Greenwood, Miss., Council leader Byron De La Beckwith, wrote to a Jackson newspaper, "I shall combat the evils of integration and shall bend every effort to rid the U.S. of the integrationists, whoever and wherever they may be," Council leaders proudly mimeographed the letter and widely circulated it. Six years later on June 12, 1963, NAACP Field Secretary Medgar Evers was shot in the back, murdered—and Byron De La Beckwith's fingerprints were on the suspected murder weapon. But the Council, ably helped by the law firm of Governor Ross Barnett, got its man off.

John Kasper, a Council organizer, welcomed Klan help when he obstructed school integration in Clinton, Tenn. Said Kasper of the vicious Klansmen: "We need all the rabble rousers we can get." A young Southerner describes the Councils as "the watchdogs of segregation in the Deep South—but when the going gets rough and they need bulldogs with that instinct for the jugular, the Klan will be there to step in."

Like the Klan's Ghouls in the past, rank-and-file Council members are controlled by rich and influential segregationists. Among them are Senators Herman Talmadge, James Eastland and Strom Thurmond; Congressman John Bell Williams, Governor George Wallace and political czar Leander Perez. These men connect Southern racists and rightists with those from the rest of the nation. Right wing politicians had labored for decades for one thing—an organization which could embrace discontented poor whites, insecure white immigrants, Northern middle classers who feel useless and powerless in a complex society, and reactionary white millionaires who resent federal regulation of the use of their money. They have found this organization in the John Birch Society. Founded in 1958 by North Carolina-born candy manufacturer Robert Welch, the Birch Society avoids open association with violently racist organizations. Seeking to unite all of the lucrative right wing organizations and seize political power, Welch is, ironically, using the same strategy which he finds detestable in Communists. There are ten basic tactics, outlined in *The Strange Tactics of Extremism* by Harry and Bonaro Overstreet, which link Welch and Lenin: 1) establish libraries and control reading material; 2) place propaganda in public places, such as doctor's offices, barber shops, dormitories; 3) sponsor radio and TV programs which preach the "line"; 4) organize letter-writers to threaten to boycott liberal politicians and businessmen; 5) organize front groups with patriotic and religious sounding names so that the central leaders are sheltered from blame; 6) "expose" enough leading Americans as "Communists" to shock the public, using "devastating implications" rather than risking libelous accusation; 7) embarrass liberal lecturers by asking them questions which imply that they are Communists; 8) send speakers to PTAs, service clubs and other civic organizations, and then infiltrate these groups; 9) organize the whole right wing movement with a dictator at the top so that force can be used quickly against any opponent anywhere; 10) "Finally, and probably most important of all," admits Welch, ". . . we would put our weight into the political scales of the country, just as fast and far as we could."

Using the "soft-sell" by telling his misguided followers that they are in an educational rather than a political organization, Welch has increased the Society's treasury many times over. In 1965, the Society expects to collect more than $3 million and double its claimed present membership of 80,000.

But despite the sheep's clothing, the Birch Society runs with the racist wolfpack. At a recent Chicago convention called the Congress of Conservatives, Robert Welch appeared with Klan heroes Major General Edwin A. Walker (ret.) and Lester Maddox. Addressing the 1,300-person rally, Welch declared that the Communists are plotting an "independent Negro-Soviet Republic to be carved out of the United States." Then, in the goblin-style used by the Klan's Imperial Wizard, Welch continued, "thousands of white citizens will be murdered in the South. Tens of thousands of good Negroes themselves will be tortured and murdered." In Oklahoma, on another occasion, after identifying the civil rights movement with communism, Welch instructed his audience that as Christians they need not hesitate to kill Communists, because "if they are truly Communists, they cannot be thought of as human beings."

And General Walker, whose sanity was questioned for his behavior during the 1962 riots at Ole Miss, told the conventioneers that there are "more good Americans in the Ku Klux Klan" than in the Americans for Democratic Action. But Lester Maddox received the loudest ovation of all from the Northern audience when he said: "We need George Wallace in the White House!"

Burrowing across the country, the white haters offer an organization for everybody. In the South, a violent poor white with little formal education joins the Klan. And richer violent whites join the Minutemen. Formed in Norborne, Mo. in 1960 by businessman Robert De Pugh, the Minutemen and similar groups acquire massive arsenals, practice guerrilla warfare in the woods, learn how to seize control of TV, radio and phone networks and make lists of individuals who will be "liquidated in times of crisis." The Minutemen have "decided that a pro-American government could no longer be established by normal political means [a Birch Society theme] . . . that there is no chance for the average American citizen to regain control of his own destiny at the ballot box" and that Americans must prepare to "fight in the streets for their lives and their liberty."

This strategy of intensifying disillusionment, frustration, fear and ignorance is identical to that used by Hitler and Mussolini, both of whom gained power with a small but well-organized band of followers. The Minutemen work in such great secrecy that most members know each other only as numbers. But they are part of the hate group establishment, too. De Pugh was an early Bircher, and, though no longer a dues-paying one, he makes it known that he agrees with the Birch view of reality but feels that the right wing take-over must be military rather than political.

There are serious differences among other rightist leaders. Some, like American Nazi Party Führer George Lincoln Rockwell, say the Birch-type rightists are "sissies," because they say they advocate the extermination of Communists rather than Negroes and Jews. Rockwell has expressed the belief that the other rightists agree with him but are afraid to voice their secret desires. With a crew including many ex-jailbirds and psychopaths, Rockwell advocates violence by taking advantage of the very principles of civil liberties which he and the other rightists would destroy.

Another faction steered by Phoebe Courtney and her husband, Kent, hopes to establish a new political party with General Walker, George Wallace or Senator Strom Thurmond as presidential candidate. The extremely anti-Negro Courtneys have worked with top Birchers, but are unhappy because the Birchers decided to infiltrate the Republican Party with Goldwater as the figurehead. The Courtneys found Goldwater too liberal, despite the fact that several government-branded Nazi collaborators actively supported the right wing capture of the Republican Party for Goldwater.

But the white hate groups' planned take-over requires money—lots of it. To supply the cash, they seek constant donations from their devoted flock. And they are successful. The expenditures of 30 top right wing groups will be about $18 million this year. White supremacist and rightist literature totaled 30 million pieces during the 1964 presidential campaign alone. Collecting the money are groups like the Christian Echoes National Ministry with defrocked "Reverend Dr." Billy James Hargis at the helm. Hargis has sponsored racist speakers and is himself endorsed by the Birch Society. He also bought the files of a 1930s Nazi sympathizer, Allen Zoll.

A profitable "anti-communism school" which "sets up tent" in big cities across the nation is the gimmick of Dr. Fred Schwarz, an unctuous Australian who travelled all the way to America, without any educational qualifications, to "teach anti-communism" here. And radio performers like the Rev.

Carl McIntire and Birchite Clarence Manion can pass their collection plates over 600 and 240 stations respectively.

No single event has thrown these supposedly independent "conservatives" into each other's arms so openly as the passage of the 1964 Civil Rights Bill. Nazis, States Righters, Birchites, Klansmen and Citizens Councilmen were all active in various primaries on Governor Wallace's behalf. Careful to flatter and, in the Birchers' case, actively to seek police membership, few of these groups have had serious trouble with the law. The California Un-American Activities Subcommittee "investigated" the Birch Society, many of whose members are former FBI men, and found it to be just what it claims to be—a national movement to halt the spread of communism.

Yet no Communist has ever been exposed by any of these rightist groups. They have detected the "Communist menace" in people such as Dr. Martin Luther King, Earl Warren, Albert Einstein, Eleanor Roosevelt, Dwight Eisenhower, Thurgood Marshall and other anti-Fascist Americans. In fact, high-ranking Bircher Revilo Oliver was congratulated by Senator James Eastland when he crowed that the name of slain President John F. Kennedy will be "cherished with distaste" because Kennedy allegedly aided communism.

Why are five to seven million white Americans so easily manipulated into hating their fellow citizens—white and black—who believe in civil rights, the United Nations, Christian welfare, mental health care, free speech, integrated education, the right to vote—in short, constitutional freedoms and the brotherhood of men?

The answer, according to Gordon Hall, an authority on extremism, lies hidden in the dark recesses of the human mind. Since primitive times, man has thrived on ideologies which "prove" that his own small sphere of acquaintances, his tribe, is superior to all others. In a large, metropolitan, democratic society which guarantees the free interplay of ideas and interests, this innate, comfortable but irrational bigotry is attacked. And it defends itself by intensifying these delusions of superiority and defending them by slavery and murder, if necessary.

Organized hatred has written long and tragic chapters in the history of the human race. But never, until this era, could violence by a few eradicate the lives of all. If the white hate groups are not confronted and disciplined by honest and intelligent members of their own community, it may be impossible for those vastly outnumbered Negroes who believe in universal human freedom to prevent the death of American democracy.

WHITNEY M. YOUNG JR.

The High Cost of Discrimination

There are some things in life which are beyond price.
No man can calculate their value. No nation or government
can put a price tag on them.

Man's priceless possessions are priceless because they are
endowed by God.

I have in mind the natural order of life—all that is human,
all the creatures of the animal world, even the plants, the
trees, the soil, the air, and the waters of earth itself. When
these fabrics are destroyed or defaced, no man can recreate
them or restore them to their original condition.

The lives of Medgar Evers, Viola Liuzzo, and all the other
martyrs who have met their deaths in the struggle for human
dignity over the centuries can never be restored. The children
who were murdered, too, are lost to us forever. So are the
families which have perished in the fires of the ghettos in
Northern cities; so are the victims of illness who have died in
the waiting rooms of overcrowded hospitals for lack of
prompt medical care.

Nor can any man put a price tag on hunger, want, misery,
hopelessness, squalor and despair. I don't know one white real
estate operator who would accept money to move his family

into his own Harlem tenement or on Chicago's Oakenwald Boulevard. There are some things which men don't do for money, just as there are some things men do for money only when they can do nothing else.

Nobody can pay a mother for her sorrow or a father for his pride. Nobody can pay a man for having lost the dignity of manhood; nobody can pay a child for being denied the joys of childhood; nobody can make restitution for human suffering and grief.

America cannot indemnify the Negro people for the long centuries during which our forefathers worked in slavery or for the deprivations of a century of third-class citizenship. America is the richest nation in the history of the world—but it is not that rich.

Thus, any talk of the high cost of hatred must be viewed in the context that the dollar losses not only can never be fully assessed but that—taken in aggregate—they total only one thousandth of one per cent of the suffering of one Negro child in one Atlanta slum for one day, if that.

Even so, the cost to the nation of segregation and discrimination is staggering—running into billions of dollars every month and also radiating out into areas in which many people do not even expect to find Jim Crow.

For instance, most white Americans do not link the rapid spread of blight and decay of our central cities to racism. But it is the main cause. Our cities today are taxed beyond their capabilities to provide essential housekeeping services—police and fire protection, garbage collection, and the like—because the white middle-class is fleeing from the "black poor."

Taxpayers best able to help support essential services have abandoned our inner cities to those least able to support them—even though the white middle class was for a time itself also "subsidized" by the generation that came before it.

Today, our big cities are in decline not only because they are aging but because their source of taxing—the very tax base which provides for their upkeep—is being eroded by the corrosive sublimate of the white man's hatred and white man's fear. The white man creates the ghettos and brutalizes and exploits the people who inhabit them—and then he fears them and then he flees from them. He builds Harlem and then he runs from Harlem. He creates second-class schools and then he fears for his children lest they be compelled to attend them. He denies Negroes jobs and then he curses them for robbing his stores. He creates a climate of despair and then acts surprised when the protest marches fill the streets and riots erupt.

Our cities cannot survive unless whites and Negroes can learn to live together in them. And I mean *together*. For unless we can share the same neighborhoods, community centers, parks, schools, playgrounds, and stores, the current pattern of segregated living produced by total neighborhood transition will go on. And as long as it goes on our cities will continue to decline. I don't know exactly how much our cities are worth—but some have estimated their value at a half trillion dollars. This is just a number to me. It is more than we have ever had in the Urban League treasury and so if I got it I would not know what to do with it. But our cities also contain the heart of our civilization—the museums and art galleries, our cultural institutions, our theaters, libraries, orchestra halls, civic centers—all that men treasure and prize. These, too, are possessions beyond price—and increasingly the white man is denying himself ready access to all that is fine and beautiful in our cultural life by his retreat to suburbia —a retreat from the segregation and blight which he has created.

Add to this cost the expense of building all those super highways ($1 million per mile) and far-flung subway tunnels to speed the white executive to his downtown office; add to this the cost of creating 100 little suburban governments around every big city and paying a hundred little suburban mayors and a hundred little suburban fire chiefs and a hundred little suburban police chiefs and a hundred little suburban tax assessors and a hundred little suburban sewer cleaners and you begin to get some idea that if segregation costs Negroes—it costs white people too.

Now I don't mean to say that the suburbs would not have sprung up if Negroes had not moved into our big cities but we cannot ignore their proliferation in part because the white man has been running from the black man.

There are some other costs which taxpayers are shelling out thanks to Jim Crow and these are better known, but I would like to mention them anyway. There is the high cost of welfare ($4.3 billion this year), much of it spent in the ghetto. There is the cost of public housing, much of it built in the ghetto, and which would be unnecessary if more Negroes could buy their own houses. There is the cost of sending thousands of building inspectors into the field every day to ferret out the violations which the slum landlords produced when they cut up all those single family houses into 12-flats. There is the cost of arresting, jailing, trying, and paroling all those teen-age colored boys for purse snatching because they can't find work. There is the cost of all those water shortages—like the ones affecting northern New Jersey and New York City—in part because slum families don't have a dime to put in that washer in the leaky faucet. There is also the cost of bussing colored children to integrated schools because so many white families are afraid of integration. And there is the cost of carrying out all those colored folks from burning buildings when the slums catch fire. And what cities spend on killing rats and roaches, on curing TB cases, and on fixing up sick kids who shouldn't have been sick in the first place, I can't say—but it must be plenty.

So far, we have discussed only the petty cash items. One of the most sizable costs has been the steady drain on our federal tax dollars to make friends with foreigners who insist on being suspicious of us. In the last decade, we've probably shelled out $30 billion in foreign aid to win the affections of people, most of them colored, who would love us if only we would just treat their American cousins like we do everybody else. And even all our "hush money" doesn't stop them from throwing bottles of ink at our embassies and burning down our USIA libraries every time an Alabama sheriff hits a colored lady with a club. I think the best way for us to inspire respect among the nations of the world is somehow to prevent colored ladies from getting hit on the head with clubs. Every time that happens, billions of dollars leave the country injuring our balance of payments, and there is no way we can estimate the pain on the face of the secretary of the treasury as the gold supply dwindles at Fort Knox. President Johnson has asked Americans to spend their money on "see America" vacations this summer because of our declining gold reserves. Lots of patriotic white people won't get to Paris this summer because Jim Crow has helped cut into our gold reserve by clubbing people in Alabama. If it's any consolation, we're not the only ones who are taking a beating.

Another big item in the Bigotry Budget is the cost of unemployment and underemployment. Since white educators don't care much about black children and push them out of school or teach them in third-class schools, not enough of us grow up fit to work in the better technical and professional jobs. So across the country a situation has developed where 11.6 per cent of all white men are working in such jobs compared to only 4.4 per cent of black men.

One consequence of this is that big business today is complaining that it can't find enough qualified engineers and scientists and administrators—at dreadful costs to their operations. Of course, they can't! Many of the businessmen who can't find Negro college graduates are sitting on school boards which are doing their best to prevent Negroes from learning anything.

Today, Negroes are taking home something over $20 billion a year in wages. Their median yearly family income of $3,233 is only about half that of the average white income which is $5,835. So if Negroes were allowed the same opportunities to work at the same kinds of jobs as white people, and to take home the same money, their take-home pay would double to about $40 billion a year. So discrimination in the schools and in employment costs us $20 billion a year.

Phrased another way, this $20 billion we are losing is the equivalent of all U.S. exports abroad with all the 130 nations of the world. Some say that three million Americans are employed in their jobs because of trade abroad. Well, by doubling Negro purchasing power, you could get the same effect as if you doubled exports and probably put another three million men to work!

In the opinion of W. W. Heller, chairman of the President's Council of Economic Advisors, lifting their income to that of whites would *double* our current rate of economic growth from 2.5 per cent to 5 per cent annually.

Compare this with the tax cut, which authorities hope might increase our growth rate by one half of one per cent!

A survey by the Urban League revealed that, if the non-white labor force earned as much as their white counterparts, Negroes would spend an additional $3.6 billion on food; $1.7 billion on clothing; $1.5 billion on housing; $1.3 billion on household operation; $1.2 billion on cars and transportation; $1.2 billion on recreation and amusement; $500 million more on utilities; and $800 million more on personal care and miscellaneous items.

After the beatings of Freedom Riders in 1961, capital investment in Birmingham fell off by $67 million in just two years. Snyder M. Smyer, president of the Birmingham Chamber of Commerce, told a *Wall Street Journal* reporter that businessmen became convinced "the state's industrial and commercial growth will be stunted for months, or years." (And since the 1964 riots, businessmen in Vulcan's City may be talking in terms of decades.)

If Governor Wallace's appeal for "segregation forever" gains favor in the North, residents of New York and Chicago might wake up one morning to find themselves reading editorials like this one from the *Montgomery Advertiser:*

"The police dereliction in Birmingham probably shrank business in every firm in the city. There are a lot of fundamental reasons why city and state cannot tolerate violence in any circumstance. But the most obvious reason is that riotous conditions blight profits and payrolls—and, politically, make the South's plight worse than before."

Another Alabama paper, the *Anniston Star,* editorialized:

". . . unless we can get more protection from our constituted officers of the law in our cities and counties, we might as well close up our Chambers of Commerce and similar institutions; for no thoughtful person wants to come to a place where both human and property rights are held in such low repute."

Complained one Birmingham resident on this score: "We lost ourselves a generation; they (young people) just don't want to put up with all this racial strife."

Birmingham lost not only the flower of its youth, but jobs declined from 246,000 in 1957 to 228,000 in 1963 under the hammer blows of repeated racial outbursts against segregation Wallace-style.

Tales of business crippled by racial unrest are legion, particularly in the South, although Harlem and Philadelphia and Paterson, N.J., officials can also attest to this fact.

In Jackson, Mississippi, chain store sales dropped between

40 to 60 per cent during last year's protests. In Charleston, South Carolina, business along thriving King Street fell by as much as 50 per cent. And New Orleans lost an estimated $4 million in business when the American Legion two years ago shifted its convention to Miami Beach because of the lack of decent lodgings for Negro veterans.

In "The Price We Pay," a recent eye-opening report made by the Southern Regional Council of Atlanta and B'nai B'rith's Anti-Defamation League, the "invisible" cost of hatred appears written on the wall in red ink.

This study puts the cost of employment bias alone at $30 billion annually, citing Dr. Joseph Airov of Atlanta's Emory University's economics department as its source. Ironically, the loss in personal income hits the southeastern states hardest, he says.

Rep. Charles L. Weltner (Dem., Ga.) figures his state would gain an extra $500 million a year if Negroes were paid like whites.

That's one reason the brightest Negro pupils flock northward as soon as they can get out. In New Orleans, a cockpit of strife over school integration, 750 of the brightest Negro boys are attending St. Augustine's School. Their counselor, Father Joseph Messina, says that more than 60 per cent of the school's graduates go North for higher learning—and that 50 per cent do not come back.

Small wonder personnel officers for Boeing Aircraft and Kaiser Aluminum companies there complain they can't find skilled Negro help as in other cities.

And New Orleans is by no means unique. A survey by the *Nashville Tennessean* revealed the state is being drained of 20,000 young people annually—wasting $200 million in tax dollars paid out to school them. One big reason: Jim Crow.

In short, we could fill a telephone book with tales of what cities have lost owing to racial hatred. It is important to bear in mind, however, that these losses are not confined to the South. In some ways, the South is moving ahead faster than the North. In ten years, Atlanta could be way ahead of Pittsburgh unless sweeping reforms are made.

A survey by the National Urban League of 68 cities found that the median income of Negroes fell below $4,000 a year in 21 cities, and among them were "Northern cities" such as Cincinnati, Pittsburgh, and Peoria, Springfield and Champaign-Urbana, in Illinois; Providence, R.I.; and Western cities like Phoenix, Wichita, and Tulsa. I point this out to illustrate that not only is suffering and squalor widespread in all our cities, but also to highlight the fact that the depressed condition of the Negro minority is holding back the progress and prosperity of all their citizens.

White people, particularly trade union officials, must stop looking at Negroes as competitors and begin seeing us as contributors. We don't just want to compete. We want to *contribute*. We built the South and we are building today, wherever one turns and looks. But unless more of us get the opportunity to get quality schooling and quality training and quality jobs, we are not going to be using our full potential— and America will be the less for it.

So I repeat what I have said before: We must march to the libraries as well as to the picket lines; we must march to the museums and art galleries and places where we learn as well as in the streets. We must accelerate our fight for quality, integrated education because if we fail in this, we fail in all. Civil rights laws are great. They will speed the end of discrimination in industry. But a law is not going to make any man a nuclear physicist. This we have got to do ourselves.

That's why the Urban League's affiliates in 72 cities continuously hammer away at the need for keeping Johnny in school. That's why Urban Leaguers are mounting job-training programs with federal aid in Cleveland, Buffalo,

Pittsburgh and other cities. That's why we set up a National Skills Bank not only to find qualified people for good jobs but to identify the number of men who don't have such skills and need to be retrained.

I said at the beginning that the nation could never repay Negroes for what we have suffered. I am convinced of this. But I also believe that for a brief period of time it can mount a National Marshall Plan to help us the way Western Europe was helped after World War II. For a time we ought to have families of the poor receiving federal subsidies to boost income levels to the point where they can break the poverty cycle. Families that can't afford books aren't going to teach their children to read. Families without enough food on the table aren't going to rear children who are in condition to learn much in school.

The federal, local and state governments, private philanthropies and non-profit agencies of all kinds will have to team up to help us overcome the centuries of deprivation. If the cost of this is $10 billion or $20 billion a year, I say pay it. Even in the short run it will bring to us a saving from what goes down the financial rat hole due to the high cost of discrimination and segregation. A nation which can afford $20 billion to put a man on the moon can do as much to help Negro citizens stand on their own two feet right here on earth. This is not charity, only fundamental justice, a kind of G.I. Bill of Rights for a people who are each day pulling themselves up by their own bootstraps at an ever increasing speed but who have a long, long way to go.

CARL T. ROWAN

No Whitewash for U.S. Abroad

No man will treat with indifference the principle of race. It is the key of history, and why history is so often confused is that it has been written by men who were ignorant of this principle and all the knowledge it involves. . . . Benjamin Disraeli, 1880.

No man in my job could wisely afford for a moment to "treat with indifference the principle of race."

Each day that I direct the United States Information Agency and its many-sided effort to "sell America" and to explain American actions and principles to the world, I see stark evidence that Disraeli was correct: race is the key to history.

It is the key to this country's future in a world where a couple of billion black, brown and yellow people have risen up in an explosive revolution, determined to cast off political bondage as well as the shackles of poverty, illiteracy and illness that are the trappings of second class status.

Race—or the question of whether our generation of men has learned enough to surmount the differences of race—is also the key to the fateful issue of war and peace.

In one of my first speeches as a government official—before

an Urban League audience at Howard University in March, 1961—I said: "If you ask me what I would like most to see happen in world affairs today, I would not give top priority to a disarmament agreement or a settlement of the Berlin dispute or any such thing. I would give top priority to having it demonstrated that, beyond any doubt, a bi-racial or multi-racial society can exist with harmony and mutual respect. I feel that long after conflict between the West and Soviet communism has faded we shall still be plagued by this issue of race."

Common, even before the Sino-Soviet split became evident, was talk such as: "In a few years we may have to join the Russians to fight the Chinese." And in 1961, the magnitude of racial feeling in Britain, the depth of feeling over caste and color in India, the obvious enmity between Negroes and Arabs in such places as the Sudan all lent support to my convictions that race was an international problem not to be taken lightly.

What I have seen in the four years since has strengthened my conviction that racial bitterness and bigotry, that racial arrogance ingrained over generations, is the ugly and ominous time bomb that spells danger to mankind. What I have seen in four years as a government official has caused me to understand more acutely than ever before the grim fact that the United States' most critical domestic problem is also one of our most worrisome international problems.

That is why the civil rights "revolution" in America can never be merely a *Negro* revolution. Whether white Americans will it so or not, their futures, their hopes, their children's well-being, are caught up in the racial turmoil that engulfs our land and runs its corrosive influences across the conscience of every continent.

This is a revolution that affects every white American because, as President Johnson said in his historic voting rights address before a Joint Session of Congress:

"In our time we have come to live with the moments of great crisis. Our lives have been marked with debate about great issues, issues of war and peace, issues of prosperity and depression. But rarely in any time does an issue lay bare the secret heart of America itself. Rarely are we met with a challenge, not to our growth or abundance, or our welfare or our security, but rather to the values and the purposes and the meaning of our beloved nation.

"The issue of equal rights for American Negroes is such an issue. And should we defeat every enemy, and should we double our wealth and conquer the stars and still be unequal to this issue, then we will have failed as a people and as a nation."

America's racial revolution affects every white citizen because the leadership of Western civilization as a whole is under intense challenge in the world today. In an era where Western wealth and military power are of themselves not enough to guarantee the survival of Western leadership, the future hangs on our ability to breathe enough life into the ideal of equal justice under law to fire the imaginations of the world's angry masses in order that they might believe our society worthy of respect, and perhaps emulation.

We have paid a harsh price throughout the world in recent years for the outbreaks of racial conflict in our country. There are remote areas of the world where "Little Rock" and "Selma" are more familiar names than Chicago or Washington, D.C.—and for the simple reason that the first two cities have been the focus of highly publicized events that were "gut issues" to the dark inhabitants of these remote areas.

My tenure as Ambassador to Finland was one of many delights and pleasures, but there was one routine that I dreaded: getting up morning after morning to find a half dozen newspapers full of headlines and photographs of racial violence in Birmingham—of police dogs, fire hoses, mass arrests and assorted commentaries about "police barbarity."

Finnish newspapers were sharp in their denunciation of "America's shame," and I soon discovered that no explanation, however logical, was a match for the sheer emotional impact of one particularly offensive photograph: that of a policeman holding a Negro woman to the ground by pressing his knee on her throat.

Seeing the angry and damaging reaction among the fair-haired, blue-eyed Nordics of Scandinavia, I scarcely had to guess what the reaction was among the colored peoples of the world.

I later saw some samples: "Billions of U.S. dollars spent for aid and propaganda are useless when the world hears of this preposterous discrimination," said a newspaper in Cairo.

In generally friendly Nigeria, the *Morning Post* said: "President Kennedy must be feeling quite small, not only in the eyes of the Russians who have always been taught to disbelieve every American anyway, but before all the world to whom he has always represented his country as the champion of liberty . . . The brutes of Alabama, after all, knocked the bottom out of all these preachments about the free world which America regards as its image . . . By the work of her hands in the Deep South, America is building herself up as the most barbarian state in the world."

The best that could be said of us in Africa that season was said in Ethiopia, when a daily paper admitted, "at least the U.S. is not hiding anything." It was the sending of federal troops to Alabama that changed the headlines from the violence and the jailings. "U.S. Troops in Alabama," headlined the Nigerian press. "Kennedy Does It Fine!"

The passage of the Civil Rights Bill by the Senate in 1964 was a major victory for the U.S. in its attempts to develop a hospitable atmosphere for the conduct of foreign policy in areas populated by colored peoples.

"By the passage of the bill," wrote Nigeria's *Daily Telegraph*, "the American people have shown in strong terms that when the choice is between honor and infamy, they will choose the cause of honor, the only one worthy of those who claim they hold the key to democracy."

The *East African Standard* commented that "endorsement by the Senate of the bill must have been welcomed with relief not only by the majority of Americans at home but also by those whose job it is to project American policies and influence abroad."

Along with explaining to the world such things as our policies in Vietnam, the Dominican Republic, Berlin and elsewhere, it fell to my lot 16 months ago to direct USIA's efforts to create a better world-wide understanding of race relations in the United States. Our task has been not to whitewash the situation, for it is obvious that incidents of racial discrimination in our open society could not be hidden no matter how desperately some Americans might want them hidden. So what we have done is to present an honest picture of an America struggling as no society ever struggled to erase these invidious discriminations based on such incidental facts as race, color, national origin, religion. We have tried to have the world understand that the story of racial development in America is not simply a story of klansmen, church bombings and murder on our highways, but also many tender, inspiring stories of great physical and moral courage on the part of Americans, black and white.

The one thing that has been constantly obvious is that this is one job USIA cannot do with any Madison Avenue hocus pocus. In no area of our endeavors is it more evident than in this field of race relations that through our media we can project the American image, but we cannot create it. Here, it is the businessman in Chicago, the schoolboard chairman in Houston, or the pool hall loiterer in Podunk who has the capacity to say and do the things that make for America a good or bad "image."

Fortunately, the Federal Government is also a strong force

in this area, and in the last several years has played a most constructive role.

I recall that in 1963 one Cairo newspaper noted that "Enlightened elements in the U.S.A. are taking under the leadership of President Kennedy and his administration, a position that reveals this understanding of general developments, the direction of world currents, and U.S. interest." Another Middle Eastern newspaper, praising the role of the U.S. Government in keeping James Meredith in the University of Mississippi asked: "Is there any other state that would spend $5 million to enable one of its citizens to obtain his rights?"

The same identity of colored peoples abroad with the American Negro's fate was expressed in the aftermath of Selma's tragic events, and the reputation of the U.S. rose to perhaps its highest point.

Said the *Free Press Journal* of Bombay: "Selma may well go down in American history as the last great barrier to civilization and freedom in the United States."

"The Government is doing its best to make all Americans equal before the law and the freedom fighters are winning the battle by non-violent means," said the *Ethiopian Herald*. "President Johnson is leading the Negro revolution from the top as Dr. Martin Luther King is leading it from below. White Americans have joined hands with their Negro brothers in the protest marches . . . Victory is in sight and the 'Great Society' is being insured for a better tomorrow."

Tunisia's *Petit Matin* described the Federal Government's application of the civil rights law as "an expression of the will of the American people." The *Tanganyika Standard* incorporated in an editorial Dr. King's description of the President's voting rights speech as "one of the most eloquent, unequivocal, and passionate pleas for human rights ever made by a President of the U.S." And in Colombia, the liberal *El Espectador* said:

"Today's events reflect the unforgettable vigor and extraordinary decision of President John F. Kennedy," whose work is now being directed by "one who, born in the midst of these prejudices, has surmounted them fully to place himself in a position historically correct for the president of the most powerful democracy in the world: Lyndon Johnson."

How will the world look at the United States next year . . . 20 years from now?

The answer to that question depends on how forthright and courageous the American people are in responding to this leadership from the government. A president can make for his country a declaration of integrity, but only the citizens of that country can infuse the declaration with the substance of life. Man's future, not 20 years from now but for as far ahead as men of great vision dare look, may be determined in large measure by whether or not the American people meet these new principles of race or, as Disraeli warned against, whether they "treat them lightly."

LOUIS E. LOMAX

The White Liberal

The white liberals are this republic's new power elite. The
liberals' basic economic and political theories are now being
translated into action after centuries of ideological subservi-
ence to conservatism. The designation white liberal is used
after considerable reflection and with deep intent. America is
still a white man's country; white men, and they alone, make
the decisions that actually affect our lives. True, nonwhites
have some influence, but it is secondary at best; this nonwhite
influence is politically ghettoized in the nation's large cities
and it is but one of the elements in the power melange fashioned by the new power elite. The new elite is liberal; yes.
But it is just as certainly white. Its creed aside, had the new
elite not been white it could never have come to power.

The crux of the philosophical gulf between the liberals and
the conservatives is essentially the chasm between an ideological and a people-centered way of life. The conservatives hold
that the ideology is the thing, that the people must conform
to the ideology regardless of the consequences. The liberals,
on the other hand, are apt to brand the ideology as little more
than the status quo and then go on to insist that only the
people matter, that—if necessary—ideologies must be altered

to meet the needs of the people. The conservatives say "This is the mold; fit the people into it even if some of them get mangled." The liberals argue, "These are the people; fit the mold around them and keep it loose; more, the mold must be changed if the choice comes between the shape of the mold and the mangling of some of the people."

It is inevitable, then, that a conservative society catapults men of vested economic and political interests to power whereas liberals tend to give the reins of government over to the social planners, to those who conceive and execute bold schemes to bring about a change in the plight of the masses. Thus it is that the liberals' power stems less from their aggregate private wealth than from their appeal to the impoverished, the debt-ridden, and the conscience stricken, all of whom are demanding some kind of change.

Precisely because they are now the power elite, the white liberals have become the new status quo and are under increasing attacks. Some barbs come from the old right, others from the new left; the unkindest arrows of all, so far as the white liberals are concerned, come from the Negro, from the very people whose cause the liberals have purported to champion. Further, and this is seldom, if ever, discussed, the white liberal is often by himself besieged. The new elite are apt to be of middle age and of above average education. They may be up from the trash pile but they have achieved middle class status in American life; they have both tribal roots and ties. Intellectually they bask in the bright, noon sun of egalitarianism, but at twilight, in the sundown of their souls, they ofttimes grow melancholy and absentmindedly begin to strum on their tribal umbilical. Then the sad cadence of lament troubles the land.

The white liberal is not a happy man. I know; I have encountered him in a hundred lecture halls and plush restaurants across the nation. He is the Jew admitting that he is no

THE WHITE LIBERAL / 41

longer a chosen man but silently wondering why Negroes
don't stick together and help each other and live together like
the Jews do; he is the Catholic appalled by the fact that he has
so long prayed that God would forgive the perfidious Jews
but unable to forsake a faith whose every trapping suggests
that there is something wrong with all non-Catholics; he is the
white Anglo-Saxon protestant marching along the road from
Selma while his eyes dart furtively toward the rising Negro
crime rate; he is the clergyman torn between the new gospel
he must now preach and the conservatism of the flock he
must feed and which feeds him as well; he is the businessman
quite willing to accept change so long as things remain the
same; he is the parent welcoming the new Negro neighbor
and praying God that his daughter will marry one of her own
kind; he is the academician peppering his lectures with liberalism and mumbling over why there are not more qualified
minority students in his classes; he is the politician voting for
civil rights and boasting of his friends in "the Negro community"; he is the banker really concerned about the poor and
placing his final faith in the poverty program; he is the union
leader concerned over unemployment and presiding over
closed shops and inherited union membership; he is the young
executive incensed because his firm hires only Anglo-Saxon
protestants and vying for the vice presidency; he is the
corporation executive wishing all Negroes were like Ralph
Bunche and all Jews were like good old Jake Javits; he is the
common laborer sitting at a bar and mumbling over his beer,
"I don't hate nobody; but I don't know what to do about
it."

The white liberal is also something else: he is a woman
sleeping with a Negro man to prove something to herself
about herself; he is a co-ed at the University of Oregon
determined to have Negro babies because she is convinced
that miscegenation is the only solution to the race problem; he

is the wealthy scion who dropped out of Yale to become a general in the Negro Revolt because he felt empty within and saw the Negro's struggle as the only spiritual movement existent in Western civilization; he is the Washington, D.C., housewife who can't go home again to her mother and father in Valdosta, Georgia. He is a child of the psychiatrist's couch; a man of conflicts, not contradictions: an advocate of change, but an arch foe of revolution.

The white liberal, then, is a man of power and guilt, of fear and promise. His guilt, and it is a proper one, rises from his convictions that the institutions over which he now wields so much power were born out of exploitation and injustice; the liberal fears that the taint is fatal, that his institutions are thus bound to crumble, reducing him, his comfort and his new found power to rubble with them. But the white liberal is also a salvationist, albeit a skeptical one; he seeks to preserve his institutions intact while freeing the Negro, feeding the poor and insisting that both the Negro and the poor—if they only will, and contingent upon individual ability—can now move into the mainstream of current American life. And that is his promise; if the new power elite can correct this society's racial and economic flaws without basically altering our existing institutions, then the white liberal will become not only a new thing in history but mankind's finest hope.

The far right and the far left, oddly enough, are critical of the new power elite for the same reason. Each camp is convinced that the liberal cannot carry out his plan for social correction without basically altering the structure of existing institutions. The far right is paranoid about maintaining our institutions intact and insists that all social change cease lest we plummet into communism. The far left is totally convinced that the entire American value system is morally rotten, that any attempt to correct social flaws within the existing framework is to treat terminal cancer with liniment.

They insist that today's institutions must be laid low, let the economic fallout settle where it may.

The new power elite have little to fear from the far right. Although some of the leaders of the ultra conservatives are money barons, the rank and file reluctantly favor—need, actually—many of the economic reforms set in motion by the liberals. This is why the Goldwater campaign came unglued. At first hearings, a large segment of the country sounded as if they were shouting "amen" to the Arizonan's brand of conservatism; then Goldwater outlined his plans to curb social security and sell the TVA and the people voted their bellies rather than their hysterical fear of communism.

The encounter between the white liberal and the far left, however, is a much different thing. Today's radicals are the sons and daughters of the new power elite. They are the children of plenty and comfort; they don't want either. "I have had all the comforts and advantages this society offers," a University of California student told me, "and I came away unfulfilled."

Dr. Arthur M. Ross of the faculty of the University of California stated it this way: "Studies already known to us show that a significant and growing minority of students are simply not propelled by what we have to regard as conventional motivation. Rather than aiming to be successful men in an achievement-oriented society, they want to be moral men in a moral society. They want to lead lives less tied to financial return than to social awareness and responsibility. Our educational plans should recognize these values."

I have spent endless hours in seminars with these new radicals. They are rock-ribbed, fiery-eyed, humanistic puritans. Political and economic theories mean absolutely nothing to them; they are beyond communism and capitalism. Asked what they seek, their reply is murky and intense. Though dimly seen, their vision appears to be of a free-wheeling republic, a kind of hydrogen age Populist state in which the people are the powerful. The far left call their utopia a participatory democracy; their clearest point is that they would have all of the people share in the means of production and the making of major political decisions. There is a sense in which these young radicals reduce the republic to a small, early New England village where all of the people gathered on a knoll each sundown to vote on how they will live the next day. The far left will get more sophisticated but there is little current indication that they will shift toward current values. The far left are young. By sheer population change the young will inherit this land by 1975. Today's power elite have about a decade in which to work their socioeconomic miracle. The white liberals know this and they are scared. Well they should be; the coming majority are morally incensed, restless and determined.

The strange affair between the white liberal and the Negro is yet another, tough, closely related matter. First there is the black chauvinism in the civil rights movement that causes Negroes to grumble about white liberals "trying to take over our movement." Then there is the ineptitude born of ethnic ignorance that causes white liberals to scurry around the country looking for *instant Negroes;* they are demanding electronic physicists and bank vice presidents from a race that for four hundred years has been all but smothered in the crib. There also is the truth that Negroes, on the whole, simply don't trust white people; they don't believe white liberals really mean what they say; even when white people do right, Negroes are apt to doubt whether they really feel it. The other side of that coin is that white liberals don't know Negroes; they have made an intellectual commitment to be one with a people whom they have been taught to fear and have not yet learned to love. The end result of all this is a kind of awkward, up-side-down white liberal *modus operandi* which allows the gifted, individual Negro through the chicken wire; he is lionized; the mass Negro, however, is still denied the right to be ordinary—which is what most people, Negro and white, are.

But—economic and political power; that is the thing! And white liberals are notoriously stingy with it. Even the Negroes who do make it, so to speak, find it impossible, individually or collectively, to get the economic leverage one must have to truly participate in American life. The Negro politician is a big man in his ghetto, but he is a secondary figure, at best, when the vital decisions concerning the republic are being made. The white liberal feels guilty about racism but he has little, if any, moment of conscience about the way power is centralized and then divided in this country. Bluntly put, the white liberal's view of the Negro is still flecked with condescension; it is as if the Negro is something he, the white liberal, suffers to be free and, perhaps, equal. Individual white liberals will complain with justification that they don't feel that way. But the white liberal establishment as the new power elite *is* that way.

The most serious clash between the white liberal and the Negro may distill to a matter of class rather than race. Discrimination has made the Negro masses an underdeveloped people. The thinking and concerned liberal knows what made the Negro masses into the uninvolved tribe they are, but that knowledge does not ease his deep fear over the fact that the nation is being peopled with an ever burgeoning class of poor without stakes in our society. This, I submit, is one reason why Negroes are kept out of the citadel of power; the white liberal fear is that the Negro, out of anger, ignorance or both, might kick the structure down. This is also why the far left sees a happy hunting ground in the civil rights movement; they are convinced that the black masses don't wish to be integrated into what is; that the disfranchised and impoverished blacks would much prefer to see the entire structure come down and make way for a new building. Thus it is that white liberal money and bodies have moved in and taken over every national civil rights organization with the exceptions of ACT, CORE and the Student Non-Violent Coordinating Committee. Let the truth be told: Lyndon Baines Johnson is now the number one "Negro" Leader.

The new power elite has a strong ally in the black bourgeoisie. The alliance, I predict, will get stronger once the middle-class Negro and the white liberal discover how much they really have in common. Their economic interests and value systems are much the same, and their views of humanity are identical: they are honestly concerned about the masses but they ultimately don't trust them: they fear a society in which the poor are the powerful. They feel they cannot let the masses take over.

Meanwhile, the new elite preside over an era of uneasy transition. Every hour tingles with excitement; one dare not get too far from the news broadcast. History, of course, lays all theorists low. Nothing approaching an absolute way of life ever comes into practical reality. Time is a tool of compromise and man is a creature of adjustment. Yet, this one thing is clear: things are good in this country but they are not *right;* not yet, they aren't. And were I of the new power elite I would wait a while before singing *We Shall Overcome.*

KENNETH B. CLARK

What Motivates American Whites?

This article is based upon the assumption that it is possible for
an American Negro social psychologist to understand certain
aspects of the American culture and the psychology of American whites with somewhat more clarity than is generally
possible for whites who are accepted by and completely
identified with this culture.

The problem posed in the attempt at obtaining a thorough
understanding of the American culture by someone who in
some ways is a part of that culture and in other ways is alien
or excluded from it, is more difficult than in trying to understand an entirely different or less complex culture. Among the
difficulties involved is the fact that even an American Negro
observer of the American culture is likely to be so identified,
actually or wishfully, with his own culture as to have his
views and insights colored and distorted. On the other hand,
resentment and bitterness can also distort one's view of the
realities of his culture. It is difficult to be objective and to
maintain a degree of detachment in viewing those social
forces of which one has been and is a part. It is possible,
nevertheless, that a Negro who has been trained in the dis-
cipline of the social sciences may be less influenced by cer-

tain subjective distortions which are operative in the American culture, or he may bring to his view of this culture certain counter-balancing distortions.

The Negro in America, by virtue of the pervasive patterns of racial rejection, exclusion or a token and often self-conscious acceptance by a minority of white liberals, has been forced into a degree of alienation and detachment which has resulted in a pattern of social and personality consequences. Among these consequences have been sharpened insights and increased sensitivity to some of the subtle forces which are significant in our complex social structure. Of course, such increased insights are found and articulated only by a minority of Negroes. The passionate, penetrating series of essays and books by James Baldwin are in themselves testimony to the validity of the observation that significant, profound, and painful forms of social criticism can be expected only from those who have been forced into a status of alienation from the society of which they are a part. The disturbing insights of a Baldwin could not, at this time, come from a white person who still maintains the hope of acceptance and success in American society. The Lorelei, seductive attractions of the possibility of success, acceptance and rewards within a given society are not conducive to clarity in viewing those aspects of the society which might be negative or disturbing. If Margaret Mead, Ruth Benedict, Malinowski, or any of the major contributors to cultural anthropology were dependent upon the culture which they studied for their total acceptance, it is questionable whether they could have contributed the particular types of understanding which came from their studies and writings.

On the basis of these considerations, I dare to use the method and approach of the cultural anthropologist in an attempt to understand certain aspects of the American culture. In doing so, I do not contend that my perspective is any more or less valid than the perspective offered to us by those cultural anthropologists viewing preliterate cultures. Nor do I contend that the picture of the American culture presented here is any more "complete," "realistic," or "objective." It is, at best, a point of view and an emphasis which reflect in undetermined degree my background, my training, and, probably most significantly, the degree of detachment and conscious and unconscious sense of alienation which are inherent in my status as an American Negro.

Geoffrey Gorer, the British anthropologist, in his study, *The American People*, stated among other things that the emphasis placed upon masculinity symbols by the American male and his sexual verbalizations reveal a basic anxiety concerning his sexual identity. Almost all attempts to understand the American culture involve some discussion of the role of sex in the social and interpersonal aspects of this society. It is my belief that one cannot understand the role of sex in American society without seeing it in relationship to at least two other dominant and inter-related forces; namely, race and status. It is hereby suggested that the basis from which one can attempt to understand the complexity of the American culture and the seemingly inconsistent and contradictory aspects of the attitudes and behavior of that most important minority group, the American white, is through understanding the delicate and complex inter-relationship of the status, racial, and sexual forces as they determine and dominate American history, as they affect the development and personality of individuals in this society, and as they manifest themselves in contemporary social patterns and institutionalized forms.

In his classic study of the American race problem, Gunnar Myrdal stated: "The split of the nation into a dominant 'American' group and a large number of minority groups means that American civilization is permeated by animosities and prejudices attached to ethnic origin or what is popularly recognized as the 'race' of the person. These animosities or prejudices are commonly advanced in defense of various discriminations which tend to keep the minority group in disadvantaged economic and social status."

In order to understand this and other facets of American culture which influence the behavior of the American white, it is necessary to understand a crucial fact in the history and growth of the American nation; namely, America is a nation which had its origin and its development as a refuge for oppressed minorities. The earliest colonists and the latest political refugees have in common the fact that all looked to America as a haven which promised protection from some form of persecution and oppression. In a motivational sense America was and is, indeed, a "land of opportunity" for the economically, politically, religiously, or socially oppressed. With the exception of the American Indian, who is the only native of this country, and the African, who was forcibly brought to the new world in bondage, all other Americans— the early colonizers and each subsequent wave of new immigrants—were driven to become a part of this new nation by some form of personal or group insecurity. This insecurity must have been of sufficient intensity to compensate for the disadvantages and hardships involved in migrating from one's homeland to a new and unknown world. The dominant, positive motivation of these people must have been the quest for security and status—a security and status denied them by the patterns of exploitation and rigid injustices in their homeland.

In a desperate pursuit of the goals of personal status, the diverse peoples which formed and continued to form the American nation developed a pattern of American culture which consists of at least the following basic major themes:

1) A systematic exploitation of the natural resources of the new land and a pushing back of the frontiers; a glorification of work and practical achievements which resulted in the rise and deification of a technology which has practically dominated the culture and formed its materialistic base. The personal and collective status and success symbols of Americans have been inextricably tied to concrete materialistic standards and production. Americans must boast of their standard of living, or their bathtubs, telephones, railroads, automobiles, because without these, they would be confronted with the intolerable, stark reality of personal unworthiness. The challenge of an aggressive and vigorous materialism from former Russian peasants—probably motivated by the same quest for status and security denied them in their own pre-Soviet homeland—is more serious as a psychological, rather than as a military, threat to the American ego. The success of Russian materialism as indicated by the first sputnik and the series of dramatic space explorations of the Russians has resulted in a damaging blow to the self-esteem of the American people. The extent and depth of this damage has not yet been fully appraised, probably because it cannot be fully faced. One can only hope that one of the consequences of this damage will not be the ultimate irrationality of a nuclear war.

2) The insecurity motif and status drive of the American people also resulted in a consistent concern with the ideas and practices of social and political equality and the continued concern with the words of democratic ideals. This strong emphasis on the verbalized ideals of the American creed can be seen as part of the pattern of the basic insecurity of the many displaced peoples who make up white America. The American creed, like American technology, may be seen as a device which is used by these peoples in order to support and obtain a previously denied status, security, and integrity in their new land. There is no question that the democratic ideology is an

important and integral part of the verbalizations, the mythology and the methodology, and the aspirations of the various peoples who comprise the American nation and is therefore an important part of American culture. The force and power of these ideas, however, should be neither underestimated nor overestimated.

The inferior status of the Negro in American society is not the only evidence of America's ambivalence or inconsistency about democracy and equality. The amount of newspaper space given to those privileged American white families whose daughters marry European or even Asiatic nobility suggests that Americans probably were never quite sure that it was wise to give up monarchy for democracy completely. Exclusive country clubs, the various symbols of superior status for special and select individuals, and the rejected status of the Negro—a basis of comparative ego gratification for even the most depressed or inferior whites—suggest that a pervasive part of the psychology of the American white is some degree of the "delusion of aristocracy."

3) Probably the most paradoxical consequence of the drive for status of the American whites is the development of a social system which seems, in many respects, peculiar to this new nation. Americans insist that they have developed a classless society at the same time that they contradict their claims of absolute democracy and equality in their everyday living. On the surface this seems irrational. On a more basic motivational level, however, the protestations of equality and the fact of economic and social distinctions are equally real, fundamental and consistent aspects of the total pattern of American culture. From the psychological point of view, insecure individuals in quest of security and status may seek to obtain their goals not only through positive, objective methods of work and production and moralistic ideas and ideology, but also they can be expected within the same pattern

of motivation and behavior to attempt to increase their personal status by denying to others the very security and status which they seek for themselves. In fact, it is reasonable and psychologically consistent to observe that the more desperately one seeks status for himself, the more pathetically he seeks to deny it to others. The ability to exercise this power over others may bring with it personal security and status satisfactions which equal or surpass the degree of satisfaction to be obtained by concrete efforts and production. The white Americans' espousal of the American creed is real and meaningful for them. It is the expression of their desire for equality, security, and status—for themselves. The presence of the American Indian, and the continued presence, pressures, and demands from the American Negro provide for the American white not only an irritation, but in a complex, paradoxical way, a basis for subjective satisfaction. His denial of equality to those who are visibly different is a manifestation of his desire for status, and an enhancement of his subjective feelings of having obtained a superior status. It would probably be a psychological calamity for the average American white for the Negro either to disappear or for him to succeed in translating the words and promises of democracy into day to day reality. It would then be necessary for the American whites either to find other scapegoats, or to face again the intolerable state of their own emptiness. In this sense, therefore, the American creed and American racism are not contradictory. Both appear to reflect the pathetic desire of insecure people to be "aristocrats" rather than peasants.

The sexual contradictions, conflicts and anxieties which seem to permeate so much of the American culture reflect, at least in the eyes of this observer, not only the historical and religious complications which were inherited from Europe, but also the dynamic complexities of status and race which seem peculiar or so exaggerated in American society. In this regard, it is not, therefore, difficult to understand why discussions of racial and social democracy will almost invariably become complicated by seemingly irrelevant intrusions of personal and sexual matters. The last and too frequently successful gambit of those who would seek to perpetuate patterns of racial injustice is to resort to the question: "Would you want a Negro to marry your sister, or daughter, or some other relative?" Aside from the matter of irrelevance, such questions probably reflect profound and deep levels of personal anxiety which manifest themselves in the total struggle for personal status, and which necessarily include anxieties concerning sexual adequacy. Rigorously objective and precise studies of the character structure of the American people must include a study of the complex relationship between status anxieties and sexual anxieties. There are many indications that these are closely related and, in presently unclear ways, tend to influence many aspects of the American culture.

In this regard, the common denominator findings of two seemingly unrelated studies may be most relevant. When Gunnar Myrdal found that there was a marked discrepancy between the American verbalization of democracy and the practice of racism, few students of our society anticipated that within the same decade Kinsey would document the equally important findings of a discrepancy between sexual moral verbalizations and sexual practices. The schizophrenic-type divorcement of intensely held beliefs from prevalent practices in these two areas of life strongly suggests a common dynamic base. The meaning of this should be explored and dissected in order to reduce, if possible, the extent of the pathology within the American social and political system.

The problem of consistency and inconsistency in the American culture is reflected in many areas of American life. The basic conflict between puritanism and the exploitation of sexual symbols has plagued not only Hollywood and The Legion of Decency, but our entire mass media, and has certainly increased the problems of conscientious parents as they seek to prepare their children for the "good" marriage as a prelude to the good life.

The problem of maintaining high standards and values of integrity, ethics and excellence in the face of the need to play up to or down to the tastes of the masses is a problem which not only bedevils the decisions of those in control of our mass media, but has seriously threatened the foundations and quality of higher education in America. Jacques Barzun's *The House of Intellect* seems an anguished cry against this corrosion—but probably too late.

It has become trite to observe that a characteristic aspect of the American culture is the obvious contradiction inherent in the persistence of the myth of a classless society in the face of the fact of rigid social class neighborhoods, class schools, and class churches. Future psychologically oriented historians might very well find that one of their most difficult problems in interpreting nineteenth and twentieth century America would be understanding how it was possible for a seemingly sane society to persist in the belief of classlessness in the face of the overwhelming evidence of rigid social and economic stratification throughout the country.

For what it is worth, it is hereby suggested that a possible interpretation of these and other inconsistencies which permeate American society is that a desperate drive for status on the part of deeply insecure people will lead to apparent irrationalities. The function of these irrationalities is to satisfy the need for status. The American white minority must erect many and powerful defenses against these inconsistencies and irrationalities. Among the most powerful of such defenses is the defense of *denial*. An equally powerful defense is that of rejecting those social critics who make denial more difficult.

This is a risk which those who still expect personal reward or acceptance in the society dare not take. Those who take the risk betray probably a profound sense of alienation. But the key paradox to the future of America may be that only the seemingly alienated can provide the critical basis by which the American nation can mobilize its real positives, its strength and its power to assure a peaceful and truly democratic world. If the insistence of the American Negro on his unqualified rights as an American citizen can perform this desperately needed function, then he must find the strength to sustain his insistence, thereby helping to save white Americans whose destiny he shares.

MARTIN LUTHER KING JR.

The Un-Christian Christian

I am many things to many people; civil rights leader, agitator, trouble-maker and orator, but in the quiet recesses of my heart, I am fundamentally a clergyman, a Baptist preacher. This is my being and my heritage for I am also the son of a Baptist preacher, the grandson of a Baptist preacher and the great-grandson of a Baptist preacher. The Church is my life and I have given my life to the Church, but, in spite of this fact, I am greatly disturbed by the Church, and I am confused by the so-called un-Christian Christian in our midst.

When *Ebony* first suggested that I do an article on this question, my initial reaction was one of enthusiasm. But then, the complexity of the problem appalled me.

I thought first of the many people who have been with us since the beginning of the struggle, who have fought with us, who have bled with us, suffered with us and died with us, who have been the very apotheosis of the Christian faith, straight out of the pages of the Acts of the Apostles. These are the true sons of faith. They come from all walks of life. Some are church members, but many are not. Some were clergy of all faiths—Protestant, Catholic and Jewish. Some were Negro, some white and some from foreign countries.

But what about the people who fill the churches Sunday after Sunday? These are the persons whom one expects to take up the cross and march beside their oppressed brethren. Instead, they are the big stumbling blocks, the Great Question Marks in our society. Who can explain their silence, their apathy, their indifference and even their participation in acts of brutality and evil against their brothers. They are the members of the First Baptist Church of Atlanta, Georgia, who allowed the Rev. Ashton Jones to spend months in prison under a $20,000 cash bond, simply because he sought to attend their services in the company of Negroes. The callousness of this congregation and its pastor never ceases to be a problem for me. How can Christians be so blind? How can they not see that the very Word of God has called for the "Oneness of the Church," and that in Christ there is "neither Jew nor Greek, slave nor free, male nor female," but all are one.

Like many other human institutions, the Church exists in two forms: the powerful, prophetic and dynamic spiritual form, which has appeared in many great movements in history, and the staid, conservative, institutional form, which is characterized by our buildings and denominational structures. True, Sunday morning at eleven o'clock is the most segregated hour of our nation's life, but it is also true that Christians are responsible for much of the power of the present revolution.

Christians marched with us in Albany, Georgia, and were accompanied by Jewish Rabbis; they rode buses with us in the Freedom Rides; but still many returned to churches and synagogues whose congregations were disturbed that a Negro was about to move into their neighborhoods. Nothing more vividly illustrates the dilemma of the Church.

Harry Emerson Fosdick has pointed out that men and women have followed Christ for two opposing reasons. There is the esthetic response to Christ which is bound up in the beauty of the worship, the moving anthems and ceremony which the Church has created about His life, and then there is the ethical response which grows out of an appreciation of His teachings and ethical example, and a personal commitment to follow in His way.

What has happened too often is that men have responded to Christ emotionally, but they have not responded to His teachings morally. The notion of a personal Savior who has died for us has a great deal of appeal, but too often Christians tend to see the Resurrected Christ, and ignore the man Jesus, turning His face to Jerusalem and deliberately accepting crucifixion rather than deny God's will and give in to the pressures of the Scribes and Pharisees to take back much of what He had taught concerning all men as sons of God.

America was established as a Christian nation which strongly believed in religious and political freedom for all mankind. The early Protestants who made up the thirteen original colonies were strongly influenced by the teaching of John Calvin and soon distorted his notions of predestination to justify the presence of slavery. This distortion of the faith aids and abets the sinfulness of man and society. This is the theological key to our dilemma.

The really tragic thing about the un-Christian Christian is that he has really convinced himself that he is right in his sin and heresy. He thinks of the Church as his own private country club and not the Body of Christ with two thousand years of history and doctrine. The Church for him is little more than an irrelevant social club with a thin veneer of religiosity, where his daughters can meet and marry the right kind of person, and where the eighteenth-century heritage of his forefathers can be preserved against the onslaught of modern technology and social forces.

In this "stained glass refuge" against the world, men are no longer concerned with what God thinks about their lives and customs; they are worried about what their neighbors will say if they fail to conform to the accepted patterns of prejudice and discrimination.

This development is further complicated by the fact that many segregationists are now retreating to the Church as a last refuge for their possible control and influence. They are becoming resigned to the fact that the public sector of life will be integrated by the order of the courts and Congress. This leaves the Church as one area which cannot come under court order, where they still might perpetuate their sickness and bitterness against the Negro.

Another trait of the un-Christian Christian is that he has forgotten the earthly relevance of the faith. He is so concerned about the hereafter that he ignores the here and now. The faith must have some relevance here; where the precious lives of men are still sadly disfigured by poverty and hatred; where millions of God's children are being trampled over by the iron feet of oppression; where millions are consigned to degradation and injustice, and where the habitations of men are filled with agony and anguish. To be concerned about a future good "over yonder" and not concerned about good among men on earth is to adhere to a dead religion only waiting to be buried.

There is much that the Church can do to save herself from this plight. This is a moral problem and the Church can save the un-Christian Christian if she will begin to give direction to the mind and soul of her followers and point out the superstitions which lead the racist to fear encounter with Negroes. No one can deal with the ideational roots of racism and prejudice as the Church can. It is surprising how seldom ministers and rabbis in the South or North have preached the truth of the biblical teaching on the brotherhood of man with courage and conviction. In a real sense, the un-Christian Christian is a victim of ignorance which is perpetuated by social, religious and political institutions.

Dean Liston Pope of Yale Divinity School has said in his book, *Kingdom Beyond Caste*, "The Church is the most segregated major institution in American Society. It has lagged behind the Supreme Court as the conscience of the nation on the questions of race, and it has fallen far behind trade unions, factories, schools, department stores, athletic gatherings and most major areas of human association as far as the achievement of integration in its own life is concerned."

Gradually, the Church is coming to grips with this problem. The religious bodies of our nation did an extensive lobbying job in connection with the passage of the Civil Rights Bill of 1964. Not only did they send ministers, priests and rabbis to Congress, but teams of Church leaders toured the midwestern states in an attempt to inform persons in that area, who are traditionally very conservative, about the facts and urgency of the civil rights movement.

But all of this is away from home. The key issue must be resolved in the local congregations. If the Church people would accept the justice of open occupancy, segregation in housing would completely disappear in a matter of a few years.

If the Church in the South would stand up for the rights of Negroes, there would be no murder and brutality. The awful fact about the South is that Southerners are making the Marxist analysis of history more accurate than the Christian hope that men can be persuaded through teaching and preaching to live a new and better life. In the South, businessmen act much more quickly from economic considerations than do churchmen from moral considerations.

The wedding of Christ with the culture of the South may well prove to be the end of Christianity as a world religion. For these churches, by some strange trick of fate, were the ones that did much of the missionary work in Africa and Asia. It is no coincidence that missionaries are no longer welcome in many of these countries as they attain their freedom. Though missionaries did contribute to the health and education of the people of these countries, the Bread of Life was baked with the bitter leaven of racism within and it is now being spewed out of the mouths of new African leaders who see it as part of a colonialist conspiracy to enslave God's black children.

If the Church would deal with these problems, she must do so quickly. We Christians of color may well have to be the salvation of Christ's Church, as indeed we already are. This is not to imply that we are the perfect Christians. We only say that God has placed us in a unique place in the history of the world! That through our suffering we have come to know of His way. As we have been cut off from the pleasures of the world we have come to appreciate the power and reality of the "things unseen" which the Apostle Paul talks about.

We will face the cross, because we must in order to survive and make it possible for our children to live in a world not beleaguered by the cancerous wounds of race and class.

So, we will not relent in our struggle for rights; and we will compel our white brothers of all faiths to join us in this struggle, for we cannot win it alone. As Frederick Douglass said many years ago, "This is a struggle to save black men's bodies and white men's souls." Today's activity in the civil rights movement is bearing out that prophecy and will continue to do so.

Yet, I cannot give up on the Church nor on the un-Christian Christian. I am much too much the preacher to doubt the power of God to call men to repentance. He is doing so today in strange yet meaningful ways. The breaking down of the dividing walls of segregation in the public realm by the Congress may well be the beginning of new opportunities for us to get to know one another as brothers.

The Church today is the same Church which John called

"lukewarm" from the island of Patmos, and which Paul and the Disciples struggled so vigorously to save from their own sin. If such as these and our Lord can give their lives to the Church and to the redemption of un-Christian Christians, we can do no less.

In this day and time, when all of the forces of history are in tremendous flux, the Church can speak out with clarity and vision, pointing the way far beyond the law to a kingdom where all men are brothers and where each person, no matter how rich or poor, how educated or illiterate, how black or white, can contribute to his society in love and confidence that his worth is insured by the very fact that he is God's child and that God has breathed into him the breath of life, placed him in a certain spot in history and society and challenged him to live as an heir and partner to the Kingdom of God. If the Church takes this challenge and opportunity, the whole world will shout for joy, and the sons of God will weep no more; but if we fail, some future Toynbee, writing the annals of the history of our civilization, will say that, in the hour of trial, the Church and the Christian were weighed in the balance and found wanting, and this was the beginning of the end of an age.

HANS J. MASSAQUOI

Would You Want Your Daughter
to Marry One?

Recently, an obscure junior congressman from Alabama, GOP Representative William L. Dickinson, made the headlines by telling what he termed "The Untold Story of the March on Montgomery." Giving his fantasy full reign, he described the nationally televised event as one gigantic interracial sex orgy, replete with prostitutes disguised as nuns. Although protected from slander suits by congressional immunity, the purveyor of this spicy, unsubstantiated version of the March was duly rebuked by the press as a mudslinger and white supremacist. And in the end, his colleagues dismissed the entire "untold story" as a vicious attempt to divert attention from the real issue at hand: Alabama's denial of Negroes' voting rights.

While the Dixie solon's ribald tale failed to impress his more responsible fellow legislators on Capitol Hill, it undoubtedly achieved the desired effect among sizable numbers of whites. The marchers, echoed a white *Ebony* "pen pal" from Mississippi, "were made up of the lowest scum of the earth that race mixing can produce. They were sexual maniacs, dope addicts, mentally deranged communists and a few well-meaning brain-washed people with no understanding of human decency."

No matter how ludicrous, the congressman's charges—parroted by the letter writer—should not be taken too lightly. For they reveal the most explosive and most pathological element underlying the nation's, and particularly the South's, resistance to change: the fear of the Negro as a sexual competitor.

There is nothing more infuriating and revolting to the Southern white man, and only to a slightly lesser degree to his brother up North, than the thought of Negro men "messing with white women," a phrase reserved for any Negro male—white female relationship. And there is nothing Negro men can do to convince their antagonists that they might possibly have other concerns. North and South, the Negroes' massive push for integrated schools, housing and jobs is viewed by suspicious whites as a mere preliminary step to becoming their sons- or brothers-in-law. Consequently, the classic question: "Would you want *your* daughter to marry one?" is still the Southern racists' most effective squelch for "broad-minded white liberals" from the North.

Rather than relying on their daughters' prerogative of refusing to marry Negro men, cautious Southern gentlemen have used every conceivable device—from laws to lynchings —to deter or punish violations of their most cherished taboo. Former U.S. Senator Coleman L. Blease of South Carolina, for one, openly advocated the lynching of Negroes as a means of protecting the morals of white women. "Whenever the [U.S.] Constitution comes between me and the virtue of white women in South Carolina," he harangued, "I say, 'to hell with the Constitution.'"

Often the "virtue of white women" has been considered in jeopardy as a result of no more than a Negro's "reckless eye-ballin'" or "smart-alecky talk." In the 1955 Mississippi lynching of Emmet Till, it was a "wolf whistle" at a white woman that doomed the 15-year-old Chicago boy. The rape argument of white Southerners is punctured by one of their own compatriots, W. J. C. Cash. In his book, *The Mind of the South*, an "inside job" on what makes Dixie tick, he asserts that the chance of a Southern woman being raped by a Negro is "much less, for instance, than the chance that she would be struck by lightning." Yet, of the more than 5,000 racial killings listed in Ralph Ginzburg's shocker, *100 Years of Lynchings*, most involve male Negro victims who allegedly had ignored the "Southern way of life."

Subtly or overtly, it is around this "way of life" that anti-integration forces throughout the land are rallying, prepared to make their last-ditch stand. Thus, the emotional forces which motivate the Ku Klux Klan's atrocities in the South and the legal finagling of the North's opponents of open occupancy get their fuel from an identical source: the wish to keep America "white."

The passion with which whites indulge in their obsession with the Negro's alleged goal of sexual domination over white women, and the fervor with which Negroes deny that charge, imply that someone isn't telling the truth. Are whites sincere when they express their miscegenation fears, and if so, how justified are these fears? Is it true, as white supremacists claim, that Negroes can't wait until the day when all barriers to interracial marriage and interracial romance have been removed?"

"Neither whites nor Negroes were or are being honest with themselves" with regard to interracial sex, asserts sociologist Calvin C. Hernton in his book, *Sex and Racism in America*. Both, he insists, consider it a "thorn in the side," and both, "for their own special reasons, are hideously concerned about it." Hernton documents his contention with numerous case studies, each illustrating how interracial sex occupies a significant portion of the fantasy life (and frequently the actual life) of Negroes and whites of both sexes on both sides of the Mason-Dixon Line.

Because of its highly emotion-charged nature, there is little frank discussion on the subject across the nation's racial fences. Negro rights leaders, fearful of jeopardizing their positions of leadership by stepping on sensitive toes, tradition-ally avoid the subject like the plague. Likewise, white sup-porters of civil rights prefer to leave well enough alone in the interest of racial peace. As a result of this reluctance on the part of responsible elements of both races to engage in an open dialogue on the "problem," the latter has been allowed to fester in the minds of the ignorant and the prejudiced. Today, it is being exploited for all it is worth by the majority of white officials in the South, who eagerly fan the mongreli-zation paranoia of their white constituents in order to prolong their own political lives.

One of the most notorious exponents of this practice was the late Senator Theodore G. Bilbo of Mississippi. Citing several cases of intermarriage in the North, he stirred up racial feelings with this warning: "The sad, sickening, heart-breaking fact is that happenings [interracial marriages] similar to the ones I mentioned are increasing at lightning speed every day, every week, every month, every year that we delay some certain and definite action which will stay and prevent the evil, horrible day in this country when both races will be thoroughly mongrelized." The "certain and definite action" Bilbo proposed was total and absolute racial segregation of the South African *apartheid* variety, with Negroes living on reservations set aside for them by whites.

Bilbo died in 1947, but not without leaving behind a legacy of his racist views in form of a book, entitled, *Take Your Choice—Separation or Mongrelization*. Today, nearly two decades after his death, Bilbo's spirit is still very much alive, having found its reincarnation in men like Governors George C. Wallace and Orval Faubus, former Governor Ross Barnett and in most of his Southern colleagues on Capitol Hill.

It has been suggested that the white Southerner's obsession with racial purity is merely a psychological smoke screen for his real aim of maintaining his social, economic and political edge over his former slaves. Gunnar Myrdal, the Swedish economist and author of the classic study on U.S. race relations, *An American Dilemma*, subscribes to this view. "What the white people really want," he wrote, "is to keep the Negroes in a lower status."

Whatever it is that white people really want, the hostility bred by their real, imagined or pretended fears of a sexual takeover by the Negro makes a mockery of the great American dream of "liberty and justice for all." It is ironic that the "most scientific nation on earth" should deny itself that final, crowning measure of achievement—fulfillment of its own creed—because of phobias that are largely based on unproved assumptions, fallacies, superstitions and myths.

The most fundamental, and alas the most widely held of these assumptions is the notion of a "pure white race" whose alleged superior (especially mental) traits would be masked or destroyed if mixed with "inferior Negro blood." This notion has persisted despite the insistence of the world's leading anthropologists, biologists, psychologists, and other students of man that the concepts of "pure races" and mentally "superior races" have no basis in scientific fact. Anthropologist Harry Shapiro, in a study conducted for UNESCO, observed that it has been more than 300 years since the first Negro came to this continent. "Almost immediately and everywhere," he wrote, "sexual relations were established and frequently regularized as a system of concubinage." His German colleague, Otto Amman, who persistently tried to isolate a pure racial type, was forced to conclude that "when a people has mixed its blood for 300 years or more, it cannot possibly retain any individuals of pure blood."

Another leading anthropologist, the late Professor Franz Boas of Columbia University categorically rejected the idea of mental superiority based on race. "The available evidence," he wrote in conclusion of a comprehensive study, "makes it much more likely that the same mental traits appear in varying distribution among the principal racial groups."

Such conclusions, based on scholarly inquiry, are not likely to change the made-up minds of persons whose racial views were acquired through folk tradition, rather than serious scientific research. The hate-warped, frequently undereducated mind of the Southern racist feeds on that tradition as a matter of regional patriotism and stubbornly refuses to be enlightened by the facts. Often, that "patriotism" is bolstered by a spurious interpretation of the Bible. "Integration breaks every moral law God ever wrote!" screamed Ku Klux Klan Defense Council Matt Murphy at the recent murder trial of the accused killers of Mrs. Viola Liuzzo, then adding, quite irrelevantly: "No white woman can marry a descendant of Ham. That's God's law . . . I don't care what Lyndon Johnson or anybody else says." A brief check of the Bible would show Murphy that Canaan—not Ham—had been cursed, and that Noah—not God—did the cursing.

Murphy and his Kluxers notwithstanding, practically all major religious denominations in the U.S. outside the Southern Bible Belt have gone on record as being in opposition to restrictive marriage laws based on race. Urging the speedy repeal of such laws, the 177th General Assembly of the United Presbyterian Church, U.S.A., recently announced that it could "find no theological ground for condemning or prohibiting marriage between consenting adults, merely because of their racial origin."

Similar sentiments were expressed by the National Catholic Conference for Interracial Justice. Asserting that marriage between the races is completely compatible with the doctrine and canon law of Roman Catholicism, it said: "The Catholic conscience condemns, abhors and rejects the underlying racist philosophy which speaks of racial intermarriage as depreciating a racial strain. Human persons are not cattle. The Catholic dogma revealed by God, of the unity of the family cries out against this pagan ideology."

Despite such powerful verbal blasts against anti-miscegenation laws, there are still 19 states which cling tenaciously to that type of legislation on their statute books—and not all of them are members of the former Confederate South.

STATES FORBIDDING INTERRACIAL MARRIAGES BY LAW		
Alabama	Kentucky	Oklahoma
Arkansas	Louisiana	South Carolina
Delaware	Maryland	Tennessee
Florida	Mississippi	Texas
Georgia	Missouri	Virginia
Indiana*	North Carolina	West Virginia
		Wyoming

In each of these states, interracial marriage is considered a misdemeanor or a felony and subject to penalties that range from fines to a year or more in jail. At times, the effect of these has been ironic or tragi-comic, as in the case of a Virginia white woman. Mrs. Rosina Calma did not have any trouble getting into an interracial marriage, but plenty getting out of it. She was refused a divorce from her Filipino husband, Cezar, by a Norfolk Circuit Court because their marriage, contracted eight years earlier in New Jersey, was considered invalid and, therefore, non-existent in Virginia. More often, however, the application of anti-miscegenation laws results in personal tragedies, especially to orphaned children of mixed

* Indiana repealed the miscegenation statute in 1965.

marriages who are frequently adjudged illegitimate and dis-owned as a result.

Some states compound the confusion surrounding the enforcement of anti-mix laws by recognizing interracial marriages that originated outside their own borders while prohibiting the establishment of such unions within. Adding to this confusion is the various states' inability to agree on what should constitute a Negro in the legal sense. Thus, a person may be a Negro in one state and white in another. In South Carolina, for instance, a person is a Negro if he has "one eighth or more Negro blood," while in Arkansas a Negro is "any person who has in his or her veins any Negro blood whatever." But the distinction of having what must undoubtedly be the strangest legalistic paradox over race, has been reserved by Mississippi. There, a person can be judged white and Negro at the same time, depending on the purpose of the judging. If judged for school admission, he is considered a Negro as long as he has "any appreciable amount of Negro blood," but for the purpose of marriage, he may call himself white up to the point where his veins hold "one eighth or more" of that liquid.

Curiously enough, the New World's first anti-amalgamation statute, enacted in colonial Maryland in 1664, was not aimed at Negroes and whites in general, but specifically addressed itself to white women. Lerone Bennett Jr., in his book, *Before the Mayflower*, calls attention to that statute which in part reads: "And forasmuch as divers free-born English women, forgetful of their free condition, and to the disgrace of our nation, do intermarry with negro slaves, by which also divers suits may arise, touching the issue of such women, and a great damage doth befall the master of such negroes, for preservation whereof for deterring such free-born women from such shameful matches, be it *enacted:* That whatsoever free-born woman shall intermarry with any slave, from and after the last day of the present assembly, shall serve the master of such slave during the life of her husband; and that all the issue of such free-born women, so married, shall be slaves as their fathers were."

The statute which, as Bennett explains, failed to "stay intermarriage," clearly reveals that its primary concern was not so much with the purity of the white race, as with the threat to the entire economic system resulting from the intimate union in marriage between slaves and the "master race." It seems ironic that the same white man whose professed concern with the purity of his race in general, and that of his (white) women in particular, caused him to erect legal and other anti-amalgamation barriers, is nearly solely responsible for the lighter-than-African complexions that characterize the majority of American Negroes today. The very fact that he made the bulk of his genetic contribution to the Negro race during slavery, at a time when Negro women's consent to sexual union was neither necessary nor asked, exposes his ostensible fear of "blood pollution" as a monumental farce. "There are several million Americans called Negro," writes social critic Milton Mayer, "whose pigmentation ranges from sepia to pomegranate to ochre, from milk-chocolate brown to daffodil yellow, and they didn't get here by any 'separate but equal' treatment."

Mayer's observation applies not only to "idyllic plantation life" of antebellum fame, but also to the unabashed clandestine pursuits of many a present-day defender of white racial purity, a pursuit Negroes jokingly refer to as "night-time integration." Alluding to this common Dixie-wide custom, sociologist Hernton notes that the white Southerner, in mockery of his own laws, "insults, seduces and rapes Negro women as if this were what they exist for." The not inconsiderable number of offspring resulting from such activity has given rise to the facetious, but logical assumption, that Southerners really don't mind their daughters marrying Negro men, but that it's their wives' daughters they are concerned about. Humorist Langston Hughes offers a poetic version of the subject in this lament of a night-time integration progeny:

> My old man died in a fine big house
> My ma died in a shack.
> I wonder where I'm gonna die,
> Being neither white nor black.

Another treatment of the same theme is the following joke that is currently making the rounds among civil rights workers in the South. According to it, a pretty Negro girl on a New York bus is ordered by a white man with a suspicious drawl to give him her seat. The Negro girl refuses. "You know what I'd do if I had you back home down South?" he asks. "Exactly," was the swift rejoinder, "you'd come around my back door at night and I would say, 'no!'"

Not all night-time integration takes place at night and not all of it involves white men and Negro women. "Few white women," writes Hernton, "and even fewer white men, will admit that white women feel a sexual attraction for Negro men. White people in general say that it is the Negro male who is attracted to white women; the reverse is flatly denied . . . what they are hiding is nothing less than the terrible truth: Southern white women are not only sexually attracted by Negroes, but it is they who are the aggressors." Hernton is upheld by countless accounts by Negroes—chauffeurs, butlers, handy men and others—who were blackmailed into amorous affairs by their white Southern mistresses with threats of rape charges should they refuse.

There is a good deal of evidence to support the contention that much of white men's racial propaganda about Negro men's alleged sexual aggressiveness has boomeranged. By picturing black men as sub-human they have helped create in the minds of white women a powerful, romantic figure that is intriguing to their sexual curiosity. Instead of a lowly, despicable creature they have fashioned a magnificent savage with super powers, capable of dispensing unheard of sexual pleasures. "Heck," said one white psychologist who supports this view, "if I had been born a white woman, I'd want to marry a Negro, too. Negroes couldn't pay us for all that publicity we've given them with our harping about their ever-readiness to rape."

Even Negro psychologists and psychiatrists concede that the attraction of forbidden fruit is a two-way proposition and that, therefore, the Negro man, too, is secretly attracted to the white woman whom custom has deemed unattainable to him. Much of this inner turmoil in the Negro male they blame on the general sexualization of American life by Hollywood and Madison Avenue. Both have made the symbol of the scantily clad white woman the major motivating force without whose presence—it would appear—the wheels of U.S. commerce and industry would come to a halt.

With or without the questionable existence of Negroes' "inner turmoil" over white women, the popular notion that the dropping of all racial barriers will result in an endless trek of Negro men and white women to the altar is a myth. Subscribers to this notion keep forgetting that—no matter how permissive the prevailing marriage laws—no Negro can marry a white woman against her will. Moreover, they seem to ignore the fact that prejudice begets prejudice and that, as a result, anti-miscegenation sentiment is by no means confined to whites. Most Negro parents, like their white counterparts, view with considerable alarm the prospect of being presented with a son- or daughter-in-law of the "opposite race." Far from feeling flattered by an addition of a white kin to the clan, as many whites feel Negroes should, Negro parents frequently react to their children's choice with strong misgivings or outright hostility. "I never want to see you or your white man husband again as long as I live," were the parting words of a Chicago Negro father after throwing out his daughter who had married a white man of considerable means. He stuck to his words even after the marriage broke up.

The existence of appreciable anti-miscegenation feelings among Negroes was borne out by a recent Gallup poll. It revealed that in the South nearly three out of ten Negroes, and in the North one out of seven, would like to retain laws that make racially mixed marriages a felony. The poll, however, skims only the surface of Negroes' anti-miscegenation sentiment since many Negro opponents of interracial marriages do not favor laws forbidding such marriages.

"Marrying someone from another race in this country is asking for more trouble than the good Lord ever intended a human being to bear," asserts a Negro Baptist preacher. This may be so, but there continue to be couples who—often against their better judgment—keep "asking for it." Contrary to popular belief, the majority of these do not consist of beatniks, "sick" people, communists, members of the lunatic fringe or "poor white trash." Instead, many hail from quite "respectable" middle class homes and a few even from millionaire's mansions in the East. What is it, then, that makes these people choose a life in which they must face the hostility of their own families, the loss of their friends and jobs, the contemptuous stares of a disapproving public and even threats of violence?

"Love," most of them answer when asked, but behavioral experts believe there is more to it than that. A white woman may marry a Negro for various reasons, most of which would involve some elements of love, they say. Among the most frequently listed are 1) rebellion against society or parental authority 2) a desire to prove her lack of prejudice 3) guilt and the need to atone for whites' mistreatment of the Negro 4) pity for the underdog and 5) an affinity for the exotic or a need for "kicks." In some cases, they say, her motive might even be money and prestige. Although it is generally assumed, they explain, that a white woman who marries a Negro marries "down," for the most part the exact opposite is true. A considerable number of white women married to Negro professionals would have had difficulties attracting husbands of similar status and position among their "own" racial group because of their poor cultural backgrounds.

In the case of Negro men, they list, in addition to reasons number one and five, the need for flattery derived from knowing that he is being loved by a member of the dominant racial group and a hostile desire to get even with the white man by lording it over that which he cherishes the most. Among the somewhat less prevalent marriages between white men and Negro women, the reasons listed respond roughly to those of their racial compatriots of the opposite sex.

"All interracial marriages in this country are more or less neurotically conceived," claims a prominent West Coast psychiatrist. "But," he hastens to add, "only because racial sickness is an affliction that is shared by the majority of Americans, which makes persons not so afflicted, 'neurotic misfits' and deviants from the norm."

Whatever the disposition of individual Negroes toward whites of the opposite sex may be, there is not now, never has been, and most likely never will be a popular effort on the part of the Negroes to "marry white." With the inevitable advance of civil rights and subsequent increased contact between the races, it can be assumed that the number of interracial marriages will rise. In any case, the relatively small number of such marriages in states which have no legal impediments to amalgamation (less than one per cent of the married population) hardly warrants the alarm of those who choose to be alarmed about "race pollution." And, as had already been pointed out, the "polluting" has already been done—and not by the Negro.

So far, the U.S. Supreme Court has appeared to be in no hurry to strike down the remaining anti-miscegenation laws as unconstitutional. Until that day, the Negro's impatience with these laws should not be mistaken for eagerness to romance across the color line. It should be recognized for what it is: an expression of his uncompromising rejection of whites' self-appointed racial superiority and his refusal to have his dignity demeaned any longer by customs or laws which say—or imply—that to marry him is tantamount to degrading oneself.

Once white Americans have rid themselves of their sex-tinged racial paranoia, they will have freed their energies for the mounting task of fighting poverty, disease, blight, ignorance and crime. They will also have the loyal cooperation of millions of black Americans whom—for better or worse—they made their blood brothers long before the *Mayflower* landed at Plymouth Rock.

HAMILTON J. BIMS

Housing—the Hottest Issue
in the North

A year or so ago, a Negro military officer was attached to a key missile site in the Midwest. Because he lives so far from the job, he rose at dawn, driving miles to report on time. After a while, co-workers became worried. When someone suggested he move a little closer to the base, the officer explained that he was unable to obtain lodgings in the surrounding white community.

As the news hit the wires, Americans across the country discovered that race prejudice—in this case or others like it—could conceivably sabotage U.S. alertness to a nuclear attack. Thus, in one of those jolting revelations that occur now and then, institutionalized American racism was stripped of its academic cloak and exposed for the basic madness it is.

It is significant that the area here was housing. For, outside the South, residential segregation has remained one of the most deeply rooted, most doggedly defended forms of racial discrimination.

As recently as May of 1965, more than a decade after

the Supreme Court school ruling and the consequent revolution in racial attitudes, a Gallup poll showed that white America, whatever its views on voting, equal job opportunity or other areas of civil rights, still drew the line, by and large, on open housing. Asked the question, "Would you move if colored people came to live in great numbers in your neighborhood?" fully 40 per cent indicated they definitely would, with 29 per cent undecided.

The reason often sounds rational: Many whites sincerely believe the presence of Negroes and other non-whites would tend to reduce their property value. Much of the resistance, however, is based on a far deeper fear—one involving all the psychotic phobias and stereotypes that have permeated whites' attitudes toward Negroes since the earliest years of the nation.

A Louisville woman, terrified that Negroes had moved into an all-white area, spoke for perhaps most American whites in a rousing letter to the *Courier-Journal:*

"When [our children] bring a child of a different race to dinner, or ask to go to the park with them or go swimming, what will you say? Will you give a flat no? Will you tell them about their differences? . . . The only other thing you can do is let them grow up in ignorance of the wrong of intermarriage of these two races. These two distinctly different races will be one, a mongrel race. Think ahead and you will see the wrong . . . After you see, do something about it. Flood your congressmen with protesting letters, see your mayor, and use your newspaper to keep segregation in our town and state."

The letter is symbolic. Its reference to "swimming" and "intermarriage" fully reflects what has been called the sex syndrome in American race relations. Even more frightening, its allusion to a "difference" between the races, the one good and the other evil, bears testimony to a dangerous equation in the white American mind.

Nowhere are these fears more provoked and illuminated

than in the area of housing. As might be expected, reactions are emotional and often violent. Outside the South, residential integration has been the most explosive of race issues, as recent outbreaks in Chicago, St. Louis, Folcroft, Pa., and other places can attest. And it can be said without exaggeration that a Negro, even today, who moves into certain areas of practically any American city is literally risking his life.

For all its volatility, however, housing is a relatively recent civil rights issue. It is also, by and large, a peculiarity of the Northern city and suburb. In Northern small towns and in parts of the South, residential segregation has seldom been a problem, mainly because of the rigidly defined social distinctions between the races (a Negro, for example, may live in peace next door to a Southern white, provided his house resembles a servant's annex).

Northern cities, however, lacked such clear distinctions, and the ghetto developed into something of an institution. The idea of "white" and "Negro" neighborhoods found sanction from the top down. As recently as 20 years ago, the Federal Housing Authority regularly recommended race-restrictive covenants in developments it insured. When in 1955 the private Commission on Race and Housing made a nationwide survey of integrated housing developments, it could identify only 50. As a result of this deeply entrenched system, it is today estimated that 27.5 million Americans, including Negroes, Jews, Puerto Ricans, Mexicans, Chinese, Japanese and Filipinos, are affected by housing discrimination.

One of the saddest ironies, however, has been its effect on whites themselves. In their blind terror of integrated living, they began fleeing, some 15 years ago, in startling numbers to the suburbs. But this mindless, almost ritualistic exodus has caused white American families far more woe and regret than many of them could ever have envisioned before they made their getaway from the city.

Aside from the psychological harm done their children,

who must some day learn to live in a racially mixed society, are the very immediate problems of living miles from the city's commerce and culture. Depending on how far he lives, the suburbanite must rise from one to three hours earlier than the city dweller in order to get to work. If he is lucky enough to live near a commuter line, he has to be driven to the station, squeeze his way aboard a crowded train and somehow read his morning paper between jolts of the train and the chatter of his fellow commuters. Once downtown, there is a taxi to be flagged, or a public bus. If he is compelled to drive to work along one of the jam-packed freeways that fan out from the central city, the process could take hours.

Suburbs offer certain obvious advantages, including the space, cleanliness and leisurely pace often missing in the city. But most still lack the embellishments of a true community—museums, night clubs, theaters. For all its ad-page glamor, the average suburban development is a monotonous succession of look-alike houses ranged around a shopping center, lacking completely the character, lore and color of the city. Such environments have a way of producing a conformist spirit among their inhabitants.

What caused this situation? What conditions, real or imagined, induced such vast numbers to abandon their urban traditions for so vapid an existence? Not counting those who moved for saner reasons, most are there as the result of prejudice and old-fashioned American hucksterism.

During the 1950s, as ghettos spread ever faster across the nation's cities, a curious species of real estate agent rose to the occasion. His game, called "blockbusting," was disarmingly simple. Checking the progress of a given ghetto, he would telephone whites along the fringes, arousing their racial fears, urging them to sell "while there's still time." The owners, never challenging the property devaluation myth (even high status Negroes were seen as threats), fell hook, line and sinker, often selling for thousands of dollars below value. The speculator—who may have been either white or Negro—then went looking for a Negro buyer, whose pressing housing need left him no choice but to pay a highly inflated price.

In one New York City block during the mid-1950s, 25 homes were bought by speculators for $7,000 to $11,000 and resold to Puerto Rican and Negro families for from $12,000 to $14,000, and as high as $18,000. A Chicago study during the same period found speculators making resale mark-ups of 35 to 115 per cent. In Milwaukee, an agent bought a house for $8,000 and sold it the very next day to a Negro for $13,000.

The cynicism of these speculators often showed contempt for the gullibility of their white victims. "Sure, I deal in the black market," admitted a Chicagoan. "If I didn't, someone else would. I give badly needed service. I find homes for Negroes willing and able to buy. Because my risks are high, I need higher returns. As long as white [builders] are allergic to Negro business, I've got a future. I live off segregation. When it goes, so will I."

Institutionalized residential segregation in America most certainly is "going." The process, begun some five years ago, already is bearing fruit. By the end of the '50s, the "Negro revolution," a continuing process since the war years, erupted in earnest. John F. Kennedy swept the Negro vote on promises of vast reforms, among them an order outlawing housing discrimination by federally backed builders and loan companies. Two years later the order was signed, and whites—in what amounted to self-flattery—predicted an avalanche of Negro buyers. That, three years later, there has been no avalanche has been another evidence of one of the least understood (among whites) connotations of the term, "integration." Negro buyers, it was discovered, are less interested in white neighbors than in being able to purchase where they please. If the "dream house" is among whites, they demand the right to own it. Very often, however, it is among blacks.

But suburbia is but one facet of the open housing controversy. Perhaps a far more pressing area—and one which certainly affects more Negroes—is urban renewal.

When Congress passed a law in 1949 providing federal funds for local neighborhood improvement projects, liberals acclaimed the move as an epochal step forward for the nation's underprivileged. Slums were to be cleared to pave the way for clean, wholesome living near the center of the city. Optimists even thought the act eventually would check the growing ghettos choking city after city across the country.

The exact opposite has been the case. Negroes displaced by slum clearance found themselves unable to find compensatory housing outside the ghetto. Many of the newer projects, in turn, were far out of their price range. Thus, as one slum was erased, another developed in its place, often more condensed and blighted than its forerunner. "Planners implemented urban renewal as though there were no racial issue in this country," complains Bernard Weisbourd, a Chicago architect and city planner.

In some cities, such as Washington, great numbers of Negroes were forced out of the city. In others, like Chicago, compensatory housing was rigidly segregated, creating ghettos far more formidable than those that existed before.

In a 15-block area along the railroad tracks on the city's South Side stretches the world's largest low-cost housing project, the Robert R. Taylor Homes—a kind of grim monument to the waywardness of the nation's urban renewal program. Into the 16-story, prison-like structures, the city has jammed some 28,000 human beings, over 99 per cent Negroes and half on relief. The demoralizing environment has produced a crime rate among the highest in the city. What created it? What produced so huge and needless a social problem? The answer is as old as the race question itself. Chicago's white aldermen, afraid of voter reaction among their white constituents, declined integrated projects in their wards.

"The tragedy of Taylor Homes," said the Chicago *Daily News* in a recent series, "is that it was conceived and is operated as a racial ghetto for America's untouchables."

Few white observers even grasp the emergency of open housing, and its urgent meaning for millions of Negroes, particularly youngsters. A Philadelphia psychologist, after observing two Negro boys on a recent Cub Scout outing, related the following:

"The one had been raised in one of the integrated areas of the city. His personality and degree of adjustment was about the same as any other American ten-year-old. He spoke the standard English, followed the Phillies and even dreamed of becoming an astronaut. He reacted to the other boys, of whatever race, with an ease and spontaneity that could only be described as wholesome. The other was from a ghetto, one of the largest in town. Already he had been crippled—perhaps for life. Because of his dialect, he could scarcely even communicate with the others and was constantly withdrawn, suspicious. His experience had taught him there was some kind of essential difference that set him aside from the others. I couldn't help feeling that already it was too late for this boy, that he would never be able to function properly in his society, that the longer he remained alienated from its standards the more he would become a kind of thing—devoid of humanness, ambition, self-respect.

"The odd thing was that the two, except for their backgrounds, were exactly the same boys. One could easily have been the other, except for circumstances. I felt a sudden revulsion for the system that had produced such a condition. I felt that the persons responsible for this waste of millions of young lives—be they politicians or city planners or whatever—ought to be punished, ought to be tried and convicted as criminals!"

But one of the more heartening features of the Negro revolution has been the discovery that America's whites—or an important number—are at least educable. In housing, this has been reflected in the rash of state open housing laws either passed or pending since the revolt. This year, Indiana became the first to pass such a bill and legislation was pending in Delaware, Illinois, Kansas, Maryland, Nebraska, Ohio, Rhode Island, Utah and Washington. Should they all pass, they would bring to 28 the number of states outlawing bias in the sale of all residential property and the rental of most.

It has also been reflected in the apparently sincere efforts of some of the newer community groups to attract Negro settlers. This is mainly true in the suburbs, but many central cities—New York, Chicago and Detroit, to name a few—boast neighborhoods in which the races live together in peace and harmony. What whites learn from these reforms and experiments will exert a great influence on the future course of housing in America, and perhaps on the future course of America itself.

As Charles Abrams, a New York attorney and nationally prominent housing expert, reminded a 1963 meeting of the American Institute of Planners in Milwaukee: "If older inlying cities continue to become the only refuges of minorities while our newer outlying cities become the enclaves of white middle and upper classes, our house will become more divided against itself than it was a hundred years ago."

Humor in Black and White

Even before a white North Carolina waitress informed a group of sit-in demonstrators: "We don't serve niggers here," and drew the snappy retort: "Don't worry; we don't eat 'em anyway," so-called "race humor" has helped brighten the otherwise grim business of the Negro's struggle for equality. To be sure, many of the stories circulating today as "eye-witness accounts" are of questionable authorship and authenticity. But whether true or invented, all reflect the high spirit of the movement which they are helping to sustain in times of danger or stress. Moreover, they are providing the much-needed comic relief for the pent-up hostility which civil righters must inevitably feel toward their racist antagonists. Thus, they contribute immeasurably toward keeping the struggle non-violent.

Invariably, the brunt of the race humor is aimed at Mr. Charlie, alias Whitey, alias Chuck, whose obvious shortcomings regarding his racial attitudes are blasted, parodied and analyzed. There are instances when the "enemy" is not only on the receiving end of the humor assault, but is the unwitting contributor to his own ridicule. A classic example of this was provided recently during the crisis in Selma, Alabama by that town's safety director when he told a crowd of rights demonstrators: "Don't get your hopes up today. We're not going to arrest anybody." And there was the funny scene of civil rights Nemesis Dallas County Sheriff James Clark keeping his

87

wife and family locked up in jail for their "own protection" during the demonstrations.

But even when the joke happens to be no laughing matter at all, or when it is aimed at themselves, Negroes have learned to grin and bear it. Veteran photographer Ernest Withers still manages a chuckle when remembering how during the Emmet Till murder trial the local sheriff would enter the courtroom every morning, grin at the segregated Negro reporters and "politely" say: "Good mawnin', niggers."

Some of that same brand of humor which is providing the spark for the nonviolent civil rights movement in the United States has spread to other parts of the world, according to a reporter for the Jewish Telegraph Agency. Addressing some American colleagues at the National Press Club in Washington, D.C., he told how a group of women tourists at a swank Tel Aviv hotel obtained accommodations after their reservations had gotten lost simply by sitting down in the middle of the lobby and singing the civil rights anthem, *We Shall Overcome*. "Get them some rooms," screamed the distressed hotel manager. "They may not be Jewish but colored."

Meanwhile back home, Dr. Martin Luther King Jr., who is much better known for his inspiring rights leadership than his sense of humor, continues to "break up" his audience at rallies around the country by quoting an old Negro preacher's ungrammatical expression of gratitude:

"Lord, we ain't what we oughta be. We ain't what we wanna be. We ain't what we gonna be. But thank God, we ain't what we was."

Nearly all race humor owes its poignancy to the somewhat special relationship between American Negroes and whites—a relationship unique in the world and perhaps in history. A foreigner, for instance, unaccustomed to sex as a race question, might well miss the point of this one: A Negro, idling along an Alabama road, begins singing a popular song, "Just Molly and me, and the baby makes three." Presently a white man pops out of the bushes. "Nigger, don't you know Molly's a white woman?" Without looking up, the Negro continues, "Just Molly and y'all, I ain't in it at all . . ."

Race humor has proved to be not only an effective morale booster for civil rights workers in the Dixie badlands, but also an inexhaustible source of material for professional cabaret jokesters like Dick Gregory, Moms Mabley, George Kirby, Nipsey Russell, Godfrey Cambridge and many others. The following samples of this humor come directly out of the civil rights movement or from the repertoires of the pros.

A New York garment manufacturer decides to retire and chooses Miami to spend his last years. The manager at the apartment building he selects notices his heavy Jewish accent. "I'm very sorry," he explains, "but we are under a commitment not to lease to Negroes or Jews." "But who's a Jew?" replies the prospective tenant. "Aren't you a Jew?" pursues the agent. "Of cos' not. I'm a Christian." Not convinced, the manager proceeds to test the man's Christianity with a series of questions. "Who is our Lord?" "Jesus Christ." "What's his mother's name?" "Mary." "Where was he born?" "Beth-l'hem." Still not satisfied, the agent decides to pose one final test. "Okay, so far you're doing fine," he admits, "but tell me this—why was he born in a stable?" "Because," replies the applicant without batting on eyelash, "prejudiced SOBs like you wouldn't rent apartments to Jews."

A Yale divinity student is awakened in the middle of the night by a voice from Heaven. "Go to Mississippi! Go to Mississippi!" the voice keeps commanding. "All by myself?" the frightened divinity student wants to know. "Have no fear," the voice reassures. "I'll be with you—as far as Memphis."

Way back in slavery, a Southern plantation owner lived openly with a pretty Negro slave girl. Partly out of jealousy and partly out of "race pride," his neighbors complained and accused him of believing in racial equality. "But that's a damn lie," *protested the plantation owner.* "It's true I stay with her a lot, but I'll be damned if I'll let her sit at the table with me."

A posse of white Mississippians trapped a Negro civil rights worker on a lonely country road. Enraged, they buried him up to his neck in a sand pile and sicked a snarling dog at his exposed head. The Negro, it turned out, was so skillful in dodging the dog's teeth with his head that the animal became frustrated and turned away. Seeing this, one of the tormentors spat on the Negro and yelled: "Nigger, stop that duckin' and dodgin' and fight my dog fair."

Moms Mabley tells a story about Little Cindy Ella and the magic slippers going to the junior prom at Ole Miss. Says Moms: "When the clock strikes midnight, Little Cindy Ella is dancing with the President of the Ku Klux Klan. But at the stroke of 12, Cindy Ella turns back to her natural self—black, and her blond wig turns to a stocking cap . . . and guess what happened? Her trial comes up next week."

A prominent Mississippi planter was enjoying his mint julep on the front porch of his white-columned manse. "Daddy," his beautiful daughter called from inside. "Yes, what is it, Belle of the South?" "I'm plannin' to get married, Daddy." "Well, this *is* a surprise, Sugar Cane. Who's the lucky man?" "His name is Harry Belafonte." "Harry Belafonte? Now, honey, I told you 'bout foolin' 'round with them Italians and furriners!"

A Negro who had just died arrives at the Pearly Gate and is directed by Peter toward a side entrance marked "COLORED." "What's the matter with y'all up here?" *the Negro demands to know.* "Don't you know that down on earth times have changed? In Alabama where I'm from, all the schools, neighborhoods and churches have been integrated. Speaking of churches, just a few minutes ago I was on my way to be married to a white woman. Come to think of it, that's the last thing I remember."

Five university students, a German, an Englishman, a Frenchman and two Americans—one Negro, one white—are asked by their professor to write about the most fascinating aspect of the elephant. The German researches the subject for 10 years, then produces a 20-volume work entitled, "An Introduction To The Study Of The Elephant." The English student goes to Africa and after crisscrossing the continent for five years, writes a dissertation, "The Elephant's Contribution To The Decline Of The British Empire." The Frenchman spends one year mating various breeds of elephants, then writes a paperback, entitled, "The Love Life Of The Elephant." The white American organizes four committees to investigate his subject, then produces a pamphlet, "Bigger And Better Elephants." Finally, the Negro goes straight home and fires off an angry letter to his local newspaper under the heading, "Biased Practices By White Elephants."

A Mississippi sharecropper, on seeing his white landlord, cheerfully greets him with: 'Howdy, Charlie. How's yo dis mawnin'?"

Indignant over his sharecropper's familiarity, the landlord asks: "Are yo losin' yo cotton pickin' mind, Moses, or did yo have a stroke or sumptn', callin' me Charlie?"

"No," sharecropper replies, "I feels fine. But one of dem Yankee Freedom Project kids that done come through here the other day told us we don't have to say 'Mr.' or 'Mrs.' or 'Miss' no mo' when we talks to y'all white folks. We don't even have to say Mississippi no mo'; from now on it's jest plain Sippi."

A white man and his Negro wife are motoring through Mississippi. In due time, they find themselves being tailed by the local sheriff. Hoping to escape, the man speeds up to 75 miles an hour. The sheriff's car continues to approach. The driver then accelerates to 100, but still the sheriff closes in. Finally, tiring of the game, the driver hits 125. But to his amazement, his pursuer easily overtakes him and forces him to a stop. Completely astounded, the driver rushes from his own car and raises the hood of the sheriff's vehicle. There he discovers six strapping Negroes wearing tennis shoes.

Jazz pianist Les McCann likes to dedicate at least one number "to my very good friend, Governor George Wallace of Alabama, who, incidentally, recently set a new ground speed record—running through Harlem."

An airliner crossing the Atlantic develops engine trouble. After dumping all his cargo, the pilot discovers he has to discard a few more hundred pounds. "We'll need three volunteers," he announces to the passengers. After a long while, an Englishman leaves his seat, shouts "Britannia!" and jumps from the plane. Several more minutes elapse. Presently a Frenchman gets up, solemnly declares "Vive la France" and takes the plunge. Again all is quiet. After about five more minutes, a husky Mississippian bounds from his seat, bellows "Remember Vicksburg," grabs a Negro by the seat of his trousers and hurls him through the door.

ALEX POINSETT

Poverty Amidst Plenty

In Kentucky recently, a worried father of eight found a permanent solution to a persistent problem. He had been unemployed three years despite vigorous efforts to find a job. His unemployment compensation had long since expired and his wife's income barely kept the family from starvation. Being a proud man, he still wanted to contribute to his family's welfare. The troubled father decided his death benefits were the only contributions he could make. So he presented his family with a Christmas present. He killed himself with a shotgun. His life was the best Christmas present the father knew how to give. Alive, he had been of no help to his family. But by dying, at least he fed them.

His tragedy is a glimpse of poverty in the midst of prosperity. Like most of the nation's indigents, the troubled father had not chosen to be poor, as popular myth would have it. He was not a beatnik, or a religious ascetic, or anyone of that small fraternity for whom poverty is almost a status symbol. He was willing, indeed anxious, to provide for his family. But in a society which links work with self respect and measures success largely in terms of job status and income, he saw himself a failure. He was an ant crushed by impersonal economic forces which presently trample the lives of some 35 million Americans—one fifth of the nation's population. Like the Kentucky father, they too are deprived not only of material needs but also stunted in their emotional, intellectual and social development and thus effectively prevented from realizing their potentialities. They are not as "visible" as the poor of the 1930s' Great Depression when hordes of people camped at employment offices and apple sellers traded on Wall Street. They are hidden inside ghettos, behind catch phrases and between impersonal statistics. Yet the sufferings of the poor elude charts, graphs and percentages which gauge neither a man's needs nor his longings. Poverty, ultimately, is a very personal matter.

Poverty is taking your children to the hospital and waiting the whole day with no one even taking your name—and then returning the next day, and the next, until they finally get around to you.

Poverty is a blind man seeking welfare aid but shunted like a billiard ball from official to official then plopped in a corner pocket and forgotten.

Poverty is having a landlady who turns off the heat when she leaves for work in the morning and turns it back on at six when she returns. It's being helpless to do anything about it, because by the time the officials get around to it, she has turned the heat back on for that day and then it will be off the next.

Poverty is a 17-year-old Kentucky boy urged to leave home by his mother who tells him: "Don't come back here, son. There's nothing here but the graveyard."

Poverty is having the welfare investigators break in at four A.M. and cut off your welfare check without an explanation. Then when you go down and ask why, they tell you it's because they found a pair of men's house slippers in the attic—in the attic, that is, where your brother left them when he visited more than a month ago.

Poverty is the eating of a sugar sandwich, because no other food is in the house. Take one slice of bread. Sprinkle sugar on it and wet it lightly under a faucet. Then eat it slowly to prolong the illusion of a full meal.

Poverty is knowing not to worry about changing clothes, or knowing not to look at them too fondly.

Poverty is knowing a great deal about how to survive on little money, knowing how to buy stale bread at low cost, or soda pop instead of milk for your kids, knowing that candy takes you a long way on its calories and that fat, which subdues hunger, can be bought cheaply.

Poverty is a family sleeping in one bed together when it's cold.

Bushels of mail about the nation's poverty problem flow daily into the Washington office of R. Sargent Shriver who heads the government's anti-poverty program. "Some of the letters are well-meaning and compassionate," he says, "like the one from a woman in (suburban) Skokie, Ill., stating: 'I know you're busy, but could your secretary let me know in what country, state or city most of the poor people live? Thank her, because I'm collecting money for the poor people.'

"The writer of the letter meant well," Shriver continues. "She really did. But for her, the poor still live in another country, in another state, in another city. The poor are a class and people set apart. There is a dichotomy, a sharp division between 'we' and 'they'—between 'we Americans' and 'they, the poor.'"

Out of this schism has come ignorance, indifference, even hostility. The more callous among prosperous Americans echo the nineteenth century's "Social Darwinists" and dismiss the poor as those least fit in the survival of the fittest. Equating morality with economic success, they blame the poor themselves for their wretchedness.

When the problem is not explained away in this manner, it

is muddied with claims that the American poor are luckier than the poor in Asia, Africa and the Middle East who die by the hundred on the streets. The poor—like, incidentally, the American Negro—are to be consoled with the alleged fact that they live better than even the average citizen in some underdeveloped countries. But how well do they fare HERE? Author Ben Bagdikian answers: "If most of America is well-fed, then the man who can't find three meals a day for his family is poor. If most of America has modern weather-proofed housing, then the man whose home is leaky and lacking piped water is poor. If most of America has enough medical care to stay alive until age 70, then the man who can't afford to live beyond age 55 is poor."

Nevertheless, critics of the poor compare them to the prosperous—to the disadvantage, of course, of the poor. While cripples are never asked to run foot races, the poor are supposed to get up and act just like everyone else in prosperous America. Since some are able to rise from the slums to material success, then all born in poverty are supposed to succeed providing they have the will to succeed. When they don't achieve, they are dismissed as apathetic, hopeless, bewildered and undeserving. The poor, in other words, are accused of being poor because they want to be poor. This sweeping charge ignores the fact that about one in four poor persons is beyond the age of gainful employment. About half of the nation's poor families are headed by a full-time worker whose wages are simply too low to support them. But even if it is true that some of the poor are smitten with a kind of Appalachia of the spirit, it is primarily because material success is rare among them. Despair tells them there is no hope of change which will improve their lives. Despair limits their goals. And so when a grade school teacher in Li'l Abner-poor Appalachia recently asked her pupils what they wanted to do when they grew up, she was not surprised when several answered: "To get on the welfare!"

Unfortunately, only about one in every five poor persons receives any form of aid from public welfare agencies, long since overwhelmed with more cases than they could properly handle. And this nation—the richest in history—has been spending only 80 cents a week per capita for such welfare aid. On the other hand, its weekly per capita expenditure for roads and highways has been $1.35, as if, perhaps, the country thinks more of highways than human beings.

Meanwhile, there is no National Association for the Advancement of the Poor. There are no Selma marches to prick the conscience of the more prosperous U.S. citizens—untouched by poverty and unable in some cases to believe it exists. The poor seldom have effective representation in city councils, county governments, state legislatures, or Congress. They have no great political power and thus can be safely ignored or humored with token relief. No national legislation—not even the present anti-poverty program—effectively comes to grips with their problems.

Economist Leon H. Keyserling argues the government's war-on-poverty agency—the Office of Economic Opportunity—represents "only a tiny fraction of a full-scale war against poverty. Even allowing for the coordinating functions of the OEO, it can hardly touch factors that are more important to this full-scale war than any it does touch: taxation, monetary policy, social security policy, farm policy, housing, credit, minimum wage, transportation and resource development, etc."

The OEO which Keyserling cites assumes an urban family of four is poverty stricken if its income is under $3,130 a year, or less than half the average U.S. family income. This sum permits expenditures of 23 cents per meal and $1.40 daily for housing, medical care, transportation and all other various and sundry needs of each person in the family. The OEO also assumes an unattached person is poor if his yearly income is under $1,540. Meanwhile, the President's Council of Economic Advisers estimates a yearly expenditure of $12 billion —the difference between what all the poor receive and what they need—is required merely to bring all of the poor up to these minimum levels. But Congress appropriated about $800 million—not $12 billion—when it passed the war-on-poverty bill last year. And this year's funds will total only $1½ billion. These funds, as author Michael Harrington suggests, are not enough to finance a skirmish much less an unconditional war on poverty.

Conservatives have begrudged even this token effort from the government, attacking its anti-poverty program as just another hand-out, just another dole, just another way to pay lazy people for doing nothing. On the other hand, radicals, like New York's Congressman Adam Clayton Powell, have charged the program is a political pork barrel, mere patronage for party hacks. And the Rev. Lynward Stevenson, president of Chicago's militant Woodlawn Organization, has called the anti-poverty effort in his city a war, in fact, against the poor—a war run by men driving Cadillacs, eating three-inch steaks and sipping champagne at afternoon luncheons.

Meanwhile, 35 million Americans share the fate of Tantalus. They, too, are chin-deep in the river Hades. Overhead hangs a tree heavy with fruit. Everytime they try to drink, the water recedes. Everytime they reach for a piece of fruit, the wind blows it just beyond their grasp. Thus, they are "tantalized" by unfulfilled anticipation.

Although whites are 70 per cent of the nation's poor, poverty falls to a disproportionate degree on nonwhites. Thus the median income of nonwhite families in 1962 was about half that for white families. About one out of every two nonwhite families had incomes below $3,130 a year, while the rate was one in five among white families. In other words, low earning power, unemployment and underemployment are two and a half times more prevalent among nonwhites than whites.

And so it has come to pass in recent years that those who have been hurting the most have hollered the loudest. Michael Harrington quite correctly points out: "The Negro . . . has presented this nation with an extraordinary gift by shaming at least some of us into a semblance of conscience, by confronting society for the first time since the rise of the C.I.O. with a militant domestic social movement. The role of the Negro in focusing on the problem of poverty is probably crucial."

While the number of all poverty-stricken families has declined since 1947, it has been at a rate so slow it would take another 45 years to eliminate the total. More important, the gap between the average income of the poor and the average income of all Americans has been widening. That is to say, factually, the poor are getting poorer and the rich are getting richer. That is to say, figuratively, one in five Americans are on a treadmill hurrying even faster to oblivion.

They are scattered North and South, East and West, from big city slums and rural farms to Indian reservations and migrant worker camps. They are entrenched in economically depressed West Virginia, but also withering in the fertile San Joaquin Valley of California. They exist almost everywhere except in luxurious and "exclusive" suburbs where, happily, no one is for poverty and nearly everyone is for widows and orphans. While a little more than half of the nation's more than nine million poor families live in urban areas, the percentage of poor families is nearly twice as great in the country as in the city—one in every three rural families is poverty-stricken as opposed to one in five elsewhere.

Inadequately schooled, deficient in health services, millions of the poor live in housing with limited heating and sanitation facilities. Despite general national prosperity, "structural unemployment" has plagued them more than a decade. Indeed, it has been more than seven years since the annual average unemployment rate dropped below five per cent. Equally dismal, unemployment compensation averages only $35 a week, covers only six of every ten workers and—in most states—lasts for only 26 weeks in any given year. Two million Americans annually "exhaust" their claims. Another million and a half annually drop out of the labor market altogether, too exhausted to continue searching for nonexistent jobs.

Economists like Leon H. Keyserling blame the high unemployment among the poor on an economy that has not grown fast enough to absorb them. During the decade beginning in 1943, for example, the private sector of the economy accommodated about eight of every ten new entrants into the civilian labor force. But from 1953 to May 1964 the private sector absorbed only about half of the eleven million newcomers. One reason for this lag has been a rapid increase in the number of working-age people. A more important reason, however, has been a step-up in mechanization, automation and new production techniques.

Thus mechanical tree-shakers can do the work of 80 persons.

Only 14 persons controlling 14 machines can produce 90 per cent of all the light bulbs in the United States.

Because of automation, two men can produce 1,000 radios a day, a task once requiring 200 men.

An insurance company, by installing automatic equipment in only one of its sections, cut employment from 198 to 85.

Recently, Continental Copper Industries constructed a new $7 million copper rolling mill requiring only three men per eight-hour shift. One engineer sets the controls. The other two men load the conveyors then unload the finished rods at the other end.

Thus automation rolls, crushing complacent arguments which blame poverty on the poor. As author Bagdikian argues: "It was not laziness on the part of the coal miner that caused petroleum and natural gas to emerge as the most versatile fuels. It was not weakness in the railroad engineer that made the car and truck dominate transportation. Nor was it because farmers worked less hard that expensive machinery became more profitable than the simple plow." In short, dramatic changes in the American economy have caused a mass of once employable men to become obsolete while still in their prime of life. They constitute, perhaps, a "critical mass" of fissionable material for a violent social explosion. What, after all, does a man do if suddenly his life work is not needed?

So far the 35 million poor—the number cannot be repeated too often—have suffered silently. For the most part these men, women and 15 million children have had the bad luck to be born in a poor region, or a dying or automating industry, or on a small farm. Or they may have a dark skin color. Or they may be sick. Or they may have lost their jobs after they were 40 years old—too old to find a new steady job but not old enough to die.

It has been estimated that three times as many jobs will somehow have to be created during the remainder of the 1960s as appeared between 1957 and 1963 if unemployment is to be stabilized at its present level. The economy, in other words, must produce 80,000 new jobs a week or the equivalent of a new General Motors payroll every seven days for at least a decade.

This poses a monumental challenge especially for America's businessmen who, in effect, can become advocates for and allies of the poor. Since they already pour vast sums of money into advertising to create demand, enlightened self-interest might dictate that they also earmark billions of dollars for the poor to create new markets. Indeed, according to economist Gunnar Myrdal, there is no way to achieve economic growth without putting money in the pockets of the poor.

Toward this end, the Ad Hoc Committee on the Triple

Revolution proposed last year that the government increase its public works and services to take up some of the slack created by automation. For each $1 billion per year spent on public works, the committee estimated 150,000 to 200,000 new jobs would be created. The committee also proposed "that society, through its appropriate legal and governmental institutions, undertake an unqualified commitment to provide every individual and every family an adequate income as a matter of right." This guaranteed annual income, the committee said, "would take the place of the patchwork of welfare measures—from unemployment insurance to relief—designed to insure that no citizen or resident of the United States actually starves."

Other anti-poverty proposals urge an increase in the after-tax income of low and lower-middle-income families and individuals, an increase in the minimum wage to $2 an hour, and an end to job discrimination which, according to the President's Council of Economic Advisers, has been costing the nation an estimated $13 billion a year in goods and services. But what America also desperately needs is a creative dialogue (leading to action) on social welfare, a massive articulation of concern for the poor. The more people who become interested in the poverty problem, the greater are the prospects of getting it solved. For the crucial test of a war against poverty is not simply what happens to the 20 per cent of this nation who are poor, but what happens to the 80 per cent who are not. If nothing happens to that 80 per cent, if there is no interaction, dedication and fulfillment in meaningful social endeavors, if their support is not enlisted, then the war will be very like those frozen battles of statuary in the nation's public parks. The postures will be heroic, the swords will be held high, but the movement will be nil.

In a *New Republic* article last July, Washington, D.C., Attorney Adam Walinsky charged that the nation's middle-class majority does not want to improve significantly the lot of the poor, preferring instead to keep them in their place. Walinsky argued: "The middle class knows that the economists are right when they say that poverty can be eliminated if we only will it. They simply do not will it." In fact, he claimed they actively resist a truly effective drive on poverty because it will narrow status differentials between themselves and the poor.

A footnote to Walinsky's speculations comes from Sargent Shriver. "Perhaps all of us who have been busy trying to help the poor," he says, "have really been trying only to remake the poor in our image. And perhaps, in doing so, we have distanced ourselves as effectively as the American tourist (abroad) who lives in special housing, frequents only certain parts of the city, breaks bread only with fellow tourists, drinks especially bottled water—and would, if he could, walk around in a plexiglass container breathing compressed Arizona air."

If this description is true, then the advice of St. Vincent de Paul is relevant. "Before you go out and help the poor," he suggests, "you must first beg their pardon."

The Typical White Suburbanite

Gordon Chittenden is 35, and he is part of the American dream. As a member of white suburbia, he belongs to that set of middle-class people whose family income is anywhere from $10,000 to $20,000 per year. He owns his home in Glendora, California, drives a snazzy sports car, has a good job, and is the head of a fine family unit which includes his wife, Erna, 34, and their two sons, Mark, 6, and Scott, 3. To Chittenden, this represents security, and he doesn't want anything to rock the boat. But there is one question bothering him. What will his answer be if someday one of his children asks: "Dad, where were you when the Negroes cried for help?"

Like so many other white Americans who have hied away to suburbia, Chittenden's reaction to the civil rights struggle is that of an observer—troubled because of his sense of fair play, but unwilling to break the traditions which he has lived by all his life. In truth, he is typical of the white suburbanite in the U.S. today. He is interested at times, even aghast at what is happening, but nevertheless maintains a policy of non-involvement.

Still Chittenden is for laws that would guarantee equality for Negroes. He is in favor of the civil rights bill, including its

public accommodations provision, and a federal fair employment practices law. He is also for the voting proposal now
pending before Congress. But if he is for all this, what is he
against?

"Demonstrations," he says. "I'm for them in theory, but I
strongly object to boycotts, sit-ins, lie-ins and all that. Sitting
down in the street is simply too much. Now I believe anyone
has the right to march, carry a sign protesting what he damn
well pleases, but I also believe that other people have rights,
too. Nobody has the right to sit down and block traffic and
that sort of thing. What's more, I don't think it's very smart.

"Now take me for instance. I'm hustling along getting to
an appointment and all of a sudden there's a traffic jam. When
I finally see what it's all about you don't think I'm going to
say, 'Oh, those poor people. Can they really be that bad off?'
Not on your tin-type. I'm going to let loose with a few
adjectives, all right, but they won't be complimentary. I have
rights, too. One of them is the free right of way on the streets
without a bunch of demonstrators holding me up. That's just
like that bunch up at Berkeley (University of California
demonstrators). They tied up the whole university, depriving
a large majority of their rights, although they themselves
were only a small minority. No sir! Let's keep some sort of
perspective on this rights business. I'll give the other guy his
and I want mine."

Chittenden is uncertain as to what his feelings would be if a
Negro family moved next door. "Well, I never think about it
too much," he says. "It would probably depend on the
family. Obviously I'd be concerned about the financial implications if it happened. You hear so many conflicting reports
about what happens to property values that it's hard to know
what to believe. Unless I could peg down the truth on that I'd
be inclined to say that I wouldn't roll out the welcome mat or
anything like that, but I wouldn't raise a riot, either."

Mrs. Chittenden agrees with her husband. "I think just about what Gordon does," she said. "I guess it would depend mostly on the people. Anyone that's decent and honest would be all right, I guess. I don't see that it would make too much difference."

The myth about property value worries Chittenden constantly. "We've got a lot of money tied up in this house," he says, "and when you get right down to it, money values and moral values can get pretty far apart. For the average guy like myself the house is a pretty big share of what he owns. I wouldn't want to see that go down the drain. If people panic, everybody is bound to lose.

"And I don't think any law compelling people to sell their home to someone they don't want to, is right, either. For instance if all the people who voted 'no' on proposition 14 in the last election were sincere, then there is no need for a law. I think about one-third voted that way, and if this many people are willing to rent or sell to anyone then the result is inevitable. What's a law needed for? I think property rights are pretty much basic and an individual should have the right to dispose of his own property as he sees fit." (Note. Proposition 14 repealed the Rumford Act, which made it illegal to refuse to sell or rent to anyone because of race or religion.)

His views on voting rights are pretty much like those on property rights. "Every person that is qualified should have the vote," Chittenden says. "Seems to me I remember that 'taxation without representation' was one of the reasons for the Revolutionary War. I believe that once the Negro has the right to vote the whole situation will change. There'd better be some cool heads on both sides though. That group called the 'Deacons' in Bogalusa, Louisiana is a pretty ominous development. The first thing you know there's going to be a shooting war down there. And who's that going to help? The Negroes? Sure it takes a lot of guts to be nonviolent, but a lot more people are going to die if this thing keeps up. Those Deacons are bad news all around. It's best that Negroes follow Dr. Martin Luther King. I know it's hard not to shoot back when someone is shooting at you but it can't come to any good. I don't believe in violence.

"I'll tell you something else. I don't believe in forced segregation and I don't believe in enforced integration. If schools in the North have *de facto* segregation—and it's because of dishonest boundaries, then it's wrong, dead wrong. But if the boundaries are honestly drawn then I say they are right. They say Negro schools are inferior. If so, why not improve them? That's the answer—not shuffling everything around."

It is not hard to figure out why Chittenden thinks the way he does. Born and reared in Bakersfield, California, he has had little contact with minority groups although he attended school with a few Negroes, Chinese, Mexicans and Japanese.

After high school, he served in the Navy, and because of his hobby, photography, and his mechanical inclinations, he attained the rating of Aviation Photographer's Mate 1st Class. Here, too, he met few Negroes, this branch of service being almost exclusively white.

Once out of the Navy, this same pattern prevailed. He met his wife, Erna, took a job and settled where he thought would be the best place to raise a family. Today he earns his living photographing and writing about high performance cars, a specialized field which few Negroes know about—let alone enter.

His wife's life history is very much like his. She was born and raised in Hutchinson, Kansas. After high school she became a student nurse at Grace Hospital in the same city. In three years there she can remember only one Negro being in any of her classes, and they never met. Now a registered nurse at Glendora Hospital, she has only an occasional contact with a nonwhite patient. Literally, the Chittendens are isolated from any major contact with minority groups.

"We read the papers," Chittenden says, "and we know what's going on. There's discrimination in a lot of fields, especially in employment. And it is not just the color of skin, either. A few years ago I was turned down from a $25,000 a year job because I didn't have a college degree. I know the business inside and out but I didn't have that piece of paper. That's discrimination, too, but I'm not crying in my beer about it. All we want to do is live in peace. We don't want any trouble, that's why we're living in suburbia."

A Mayor Picks a Deprived Area

For Trenton, N.J. Mayor Arthur John Holland, being chief executive of his city means more than simply priming a political pump for his personal gain and leaving the 114,000 other citizens to exist by the grace of God.

Mayor Holland, 46, is the only known white man of political substance who intentionally moved his family into a neighborhood which was 50 per cent Negro, including a number of poverty-stricken, welfare-aided, husbandless mothers with babies.

If there ever was a thriving multi-racial neighborhood in the heart of a U.S. industrial city, it is the Mercer Street area where the mayor (a lifelong resident of New Jersey's capital city) and his family live in constructive harmony with their neighbors. To the left lives a quiet Negro couple. To the right lives an aging white woman. Also living in the neighborhood are Puerto Ricans, Jews, Poles and Germans. And among the classes of people are the poor, the strivers, the little people and the big.

Across the street from the Hollands' home is a Quaker Friends' Society recreation center where his daughter, Cynthia, loves to swing and where 90 per cent of her playmates are Negro and Puerto Rican youngsters.

The mayor's move, in February of 1964, surprised many Trentonites and shocked even more. His political aides told him he would hurt his political future by moving into the 100-year-old house on Mercer Street. But Holland had faith that Trenton's citizens would not punish him for exercising, however unusually, the right to live where and among whom he chose.

Besides, as Trenton NAACP President Mrs. Robert Graham observed when Mayor Holland announced his decision, "He's known as 'Honest John.' In some things he is too honest to be a politician. He always wants to do the right thing and tries hard to do it, too."

Now, only a year and a half later, many more Trentonites have come to agree with Mayor Holland that he did the right thing. Furthermore, there can no longer be lame political excuses for those mayors who live in the city outskirts far removed from the people whom they profess to serve.

There was nothing spectacular (other than press coverage) in Mayor Holland's moving into a new neighborhood.

But there was much significance.

For Mayor Holland has set an example for other white people who wish to move back into major urban centers which they abandoned to Negroes. Too many whites have believed that when they fled their city neighborhoods, they escaped a share of the responsibility for the depressing, stifling ghettos which rose in their wake. When concerned and educated men remain in these changing neighborhoods, they keep the community diverse and help prevent the oppression and exploitation which is the common lot of the unprotected poor.

How have the Hollands been received in their new neighborhood?

Amazingly well, they reveal. But, contrary to the opinions of many who claimed that the Hollands worshipped Negroes, or were pulling a "do-gooder" stunt, the family has not attempted to become intimate friends with all their neighbors. Normal, hard-working people, challenged by the stresses and strains of any busy young family, Mayor and Mrs. Holland are on speaking terms with their whole neighborhood but close friends of only a few. The Negro family and the white woman who live next door are the warmest friends of the Hollands not simply because they are next-door neighbors, but mainly because they simply "hit it off."

For a time after they moved in, there was the predictable influx of hate mail from across the nation, but most of the letters were kind. Typical of the congratulations was a letter from a Midwestern couple who wrote: "Thanks for doing what many of us haven't the guts to do." Gentlest of the hate letters was one from a Charlotte, N.C., man who frankly declared, "You're nuts!" And a New York-based bigot organization sent the mayor a bundle of its literature claiming that mixing, in any way, with other races was anthropologically destructive.

"The hate mail is no longer a problem," Mrs. Holland sighs in relief. And the mayor adds: "We have been heartened by the people who seem to enjoy having us live here. Sometimes, I hear youths who are walking down the street call out, 'Hi, Mayor Holland,' even though they can't see me and don't even know if I'm home."

When Cynthia, the elder Holland daughter at two years old, goes out her front door to play, other neighborhood children frequently run across the street to hold her hand or jump rope with her. At the playground where Cynthia and Elise, her one-year-old sister, romp, Cynthia is the center of attention—not because she is the mayor's child but because she is an active and gregarious little girl.

Since the mayor's move to what is known as the Mercer-Jackson area, a number of other property owners have painted and spruced up their homes and lawns. Movement away from the neighborhood is now negligible, and a number of whites who had planned to move before the Hollands moved in took down their "For Sale" signs and decided to stay. A recent college graduate, with his family, and a school-teacher have just moved on the block. And the head of the Trenton Parking Authority plans to restore his recently bought house which is located three doors from the home of the Hollands.

Around the neighborhood, from the illiterate to a number of professionals, the trend appears to be evolving slowly towards what Mrs. Holland hopefully sees as a close-knit residential area on a non-segregated basis. Her dream model for the appearance of the neighborhood is Georgetown, Washington, D.C.'s aristocratic neighborhood.

Her dream may become true, someday, because there is now a Mercer-Jackson Conservation and Rehabilitation Program which is designed to restore the area to its original attractiveness. Under this program, sound structures will be kept and unsound ones will be destroyed and replaced.

Across historic Assunpink Creek, behind the Hollands' home, a public park with tree-shaded walkways and benches, is already on the drawing boards.

Far from creating major problems, as some predicted, the mayor's move into this "run-down" area is actually leading to the first meaningful confrontation between whites and the decay of Trenton's inner city. Holland has always been genuinely concerned about the poor, but another possible key to why the mayor had no qualms about moving into a mixed neighborhood is the fact that he spent six years as a seminary student. He studied to be a Franciscan priest but when he came up for final vows, he decided that he did not have a religious calling. A sister of his is a nun and lives with a Negro nun at St. Matthew's Convent in Nixon, N.J.

In politics for ten years, with six as mayor, Holland was elected a city commissioner in 1955. In 1959, he was elected mayor, and reelected in 1962 after he persuaded the city to accept a strong mayor-council-administrator form of government.

Today, the mayor's outlook is further displayed by the many programs his administration is instituting on behalf of the city's poor. By early summer, the city had received commitments for $2.16 million in federal, state and private funds to attack poverty.

Trenton is proud of being the first city in the nation to involve the poor in helping to work out their own problems through elections for their own representatives in three areas of the city. In these elections, voters practiced on the machines used in normal elections. The three areas include Mercer-Jackson, East Trenton and Battle Monument.

Outstanding among Trenton's many programs for the culturally disadvantaged is one of the first pre-pre-kindergarten programs under which three-year-olds are given a headstart toward learning good study habits.

All of these programs, designed for a massive attack on the ravages of poverty, are in keeping with Mayor Holland's announced opinion that "if physical renewal is to be successful, it must be accompanied by human renewal." Taking advantage of the U.S. Government's Economic Opportunity Act, which he, as a member of the Executive Board of the National League of Cities, helped to get passed, Mayor Holland organized a Human Renewal Coordinating Committee. On the committee are representative community leaders who make recommendations concerning the organization of a Community Action Agency and the marshalling of an effective war against poverty in the city.

Out of the committee grew United Progress, Inc. (UPI). UPI is seeking new approaches to old economic and social problems and maintains maximum imagination and flexibility in the hiring of its staff. It is financed by funds from private foundations, thus escaping political manipulation, and is able to utilize existing agencies and resources to create new ones as required.

Both in his unusual home neighborhood, as well as in the entire city of Trenton, Mayor Holland has set a new trend of impressive, intelligent and humanitarian leadership.

By uprooting potential ghettos and by cultivating healthy, natural integration, men like Mayor John Holland help both the impoverished and the well-to-do work side by side to end race and class prejudice.

PONCHITTA PIERCE

Crime in the Suburbs

Residents of New York's suburban Nassau County could hardly believe it, but there before them recently was unmistakable evidence. After two years of undercover work, police had smashed a ring of housewives working as call girls to boost their family incomes. Grossing more than $200,000 annually, the housewives-turned-professionals had charged from $24 to $100 an hour for services rendered. While some of their husbands were shocked at these disclosures, at least one was a co-partner in crime. He baby-sat at home while his wife entertained her clients. The suburban sex scandal brought admissions of guilt from 26 to 40 persons indicted either as call girls or procurers.

While the call girl ring was unusual, it nevertheless pointed up the embarrassing fact that crime is becoming almost as characteristic of suburbia as crab grass. The "ideal" communities across the nation which once promised peace, quiet and "exclusiveness" are now confronted with a crime rate that jumped 6 per cent during the first three months of this year. For example, robberies in suburbia have gone up 13 per cent and larceny involving $50 or more has risen 11 per cent, according to the Federal Bureau of Investigation. And last year, suburban crime rose 18 per cent, an increase 5 per cent greater than in the cities.

"If all the crimes were acted upon, the rate would be a lot higher," reveals Circuit Court Judge William J. Bauer of DuPage County near Chicago. "What would be a major crime at Taylor and Halsted (in Chicago) may never get to court in the better middle-class suburbs." Thus while shoplifting is a police problem in Scarsdale, N.Y., "most of it never gets reported," admits Police Chief James Lyons. "We generally hear about it through the grapevine. I suppose the merchants prefer to take care of it individually rather than bringing it to us."

A possible reason for this hush-hush is that much of the crime in suburbia is committed by teen-agers from well-to-do families. "They're always saying that slum areas breed crime," says Police Commissioner Adam Buckawick of suburban Glen Cove, N.Y. "This might be true in a different town. But here the so-called bad kids don't get in trouble. It's the good ones. We have two slum areas here. And the two schools in these areas don't have the problems of vandalism. I differ with the experts about the better schools. That's where we have real vandalism."

Buckawick also blames some of Glen Cove's crime on the local population explosion and a number of colleges which have sprung up around the area. "Now don't get me wrong," he says. "These colleges are good but the kids can give you a lot of trouble. They don't go in for burglary, but they're mischievous. They drink, raise a ruckus on the beach, take our signs. I guess they get a big kick out of that. They drive fast. We try not to make an arrest. That would be on their record for life. We let them sweat it out and then turn them loose. They're not repeaters. Once they're in here, they're rarely here a second time."

The use of drugs—especially among juveniles—has been

one of the most frequently publicized crimes in the suburbs. In some New York, Chicago and Los Angeles suburbs, police attribute between 30 and 80 per cent of all local crime to drug addiction. "The people in these suburbs don't want to talk about it," explains one official. "They're afraid it'll depress real-estate values. It'll give the town a bad name."

One of the country's worst drug addiction centers is Los Angeles County which in 1962 reported more than 1,000 juveniles arrested for drug offenses. In the early 1950s police recorded an average of only 76 juvenile narcotic offenders. Now there are more than that many deaths from narcotics and dangerous drugs—104 in 1962.

"Some of these kids come from beautiful homes," says W. J. Hunt, chairman of the Los Angeles County Narcotics and Dangerous Drug Commission. "While their parents are at some cocktail party, the kids drink, gulp down pills, and away they go toward marijuana and heroin."

Recently grade school children as young as nine years old were found using marijuana in Marin County near San Francisco. Some in Sausalito, a small town in the county, had been solicited by peddlers who passed out free samples in the public square. "Smoking marijuana is better than drinking whiskey," one defiant youngster told an investigating grand jury. "My old man drinks hard whiskey and it's done him more harm than marijuana's done me."

In one section of wealthy Fairfield County, Connecticut, reports *The Saturday Evening Post*, authorities are no longer surprised to see half a dozen or more fancy convertibles pull up on a lonely road at night. In each car are two, three or four youngsters. They roll up the windows and then "blow pot" —smoke marijuana, keeping the windows closed in order to inhale as much smoke as possible.

Pot parties and goof-ball (barbiturate) parties also flourish in the better suburbs of Chicago—Evanston, Oak Park,

Skokie. In some high schools pockets of users are the rule. Last year, police in Yonkers, N.Y., reported 140 juvenile users of heroin, opium and cocaine and 800 known marijuana smokers and pill users. Their average age was between 17 and 20 and a third of them were girls.

When heroin or marijuana doesn't attract suburban youths, they often fall prey to pills. Collectively called "goof balls," they are known technically as barbiturates (depressants) and amphetamines (stimulants). The so-called "joy pills," alias "Christmas Trees," "Yellow Jackets," "Red Devils," and "Purple Hearts" are said to be more dangerous in some cases than such hard-core narcotics as marijuana, cocaine and heroin. Addicts or "junkies" whose habit costs from $50 to $75 a day have been known to shun the pills even though they can be purchased in large quantities for a minimal sum. "I know I'm a junkie," explained one girl. "I steal, connive, prostitute and anything else for a fix, but I never—but never! —fool around with the goof balls. They drive you crazy. You have no control of the mind. With heroin, you do."

Like dope usage, shoplifting—particularly among teen-agers—is also increasing in suburbia. An example is Greenwich, Connecticut, one of the nation's richest communities and often described as the "bedroom of Wall Street." Many of the local teen-agers receive allowances of from $10 to $25 a week and generally drive their own cars. Greenwich, therefore, would seem the last place on earth for shoplifting. But the crime abounds. Deputy Police Chief Thomas C. Burke blames parents more than their children for the increase. "Parents are not aggressive enough in finding out where the new things their children have come from," he says. "I frequently wonder why they accept their child's first story. Why don't they check once to see if Mary or John really did borrow the item from a friend. All they have to do is make a call to the other parent." When a teen-ager shoplifts an article he usually tells his parent, "A friend gave it to me or loaned it to me," the chief says. Records, cosmetics and clothing are among the popular items.

"I would say shoplifting is a form of amusement for most people," observes 21-year-old Greenwich co-ed Penny Johnston. "They get a charge out of getting something for nothing. Their ideas of fun also include throwing rocks at cars or putting bottles across the road."

Party crashing, teen-age drinking, bicycle stealing and mailbox destruction are additional problems for suburbia in general and the Greenwich Police Department in particular. Deputy Police Chief Burke attributes this primarily "to a breakdown in the area of respect for other people's property." He also finds that kids seemed to have had more remorse and shame a few years back when they were caught for a crime than they do now. "I don't want to sound old-fashioned," he says, "but today they tell you, 'Mary Jane can get away with it, I can too.'" Parents may be placing too much responsibility on schools and law enforcement agencies to bring up their children. I know how hard it is to say 'no' to your own child, and to punish him, but it has to be done."

Additional assessments of crime in Greenwich come from Robert Day, city editor of *The Daily Item*, who believes local lawlessness springs from general boredom. "The kids need an outlet," he says. "They don't have much responsibility. They're affluent enough, but they don't have anything to keep them busy."

Day thinks parents generally are abrogating their responsibility. "I know I go home at five in the afternoon," he says, "and don't come up for air until 9 P.M. when the youngsters are in bed. I don't know if we should be asking why children are acting up as much as why parents aren't facing their responsibilities."

While Greenwich has its share of such regular crimes as

burglary, auto thefts and larceny, boat thefts are its special problem. With more than 3,500 registered there, the suburb has the largest boat concentration anywhere in the state. "Boat thefts are on the increase," reports Deputy Police Chief Burke. "People fail to safeguard their property. They leave equipment where it's easy to get at it."

Autos, on the other hand, are the big prize at shopping centers in Evergreen Park, a Chicago suburb. Police Chief Albert Brietzman says thieves "can pick and choose the car they want—just like going to a used-car lot." In line with this, the efficient new expressways that crisscross the nation have proved to be convenient escape routes not only for car thieves in suburbs but burglars and other criminals as well. The very expressways that bring the city closer to suburbanites, unfortunately also bring the suburbs closer to the city's hoodlums. In Scarsdale, N.Y., for example, 90 per cent of the persons arrested for crimes last year were non-residents.

"When they built the Congress Expressway (in Chicago) they increased crime in DuPage County," says Circuit Court Judge William J. Bauer. "It used to take 1½ hours to get out here from the city. Now you can get in and commit a crime and get out in 35 minutes without breaking a speed law."

But suburban residents themselves must share the blame for the mounting crime rate in their communities. "People move to the suburbs and buy a $150 lawnmower, put it in the garage, then leave the garage door open," says Police Chief Mark Orlick of Chicago Heights, Ill. "They buy their kids $100 bicycles, but won't invest in a $3 lock. In summer, women will work in back of the house and leave the front door open. Then they wonder why people rifle their homes."

Other suburban crime causes are many and vary from community to community. "I hate to say it, but today there is less chance of a criminal being caught," says Police Commissioner James Dwyer of White Plains, N.Y. "This is because there are not enough people in law enforcement and the fact that people themselves often don't want to go to court to press charges or be involved. Another thing, there are so many interpretations of the law which seem to show more concern for the offender than for the fact of the crime, so much so that we disregard facts in our eagerness to make sure some technical point—in the arrest for example—has not been violated. This, plus the fact that many of our laws are antiquated help explain the rise in suburban crime."

A continuation of this trend seems assured by the coming of big-time criminals to suburbia. For example, about 60 well-known racketeers of Mafia and Cosa Nostra fame live in New York's Nassau County. "We can't say that they're actively engaged in crime in this particular area," says District Attorney William Kahn. "But we alert the public to the fact that they are living in the country because their mere presence is a threat to our residents. Most of them move to the suburbs, take on the mantle of the country squire and practice their nefarious activities elsewhere." Meanwhile, however, organized bookmaking and gambling is on the rise in Nassau County.

And crime in general is a spreading crack in the picture window of suburbia. "Not only is the crime rate up, but it is going to continue to go up," predicts Police Chief Clarence Emrikson of Niles, Ill. "I can't see it getting anything but worse."

It's Against the Law!

An anthropologist of the twenty-seventh century, examining present-day America solely through its state and local laws, would have to conclude that here was an unbelievable land.

He would discover, for example, that in a place called Haywood County, Tenn., in 1965, A.D., Negroes, although they owned most of the land and paid most of the taxes, were subject to curfew, prohibited from dancing and drinking beer, forbidden in the vicinity of the county courthouse except on business.

Further along, his interest would increase. It would seem that in a state called Alabama, about the same time, Negro parents decided one day to send their children to schools nearest their homes—whereupon whites, out of sheer prejudice, passed a special law allowing them to withdraw their own children, even at the price of their education.

Astonishment would follow astonishment. The scholar would find that statutes in no less than 19 states across this strange country actually presumed to dictate who should and should not marry, some jailing violators for up to seven years; that in Oklahoma, although Negro passengers paid the same fare as whites, they were forbidden to occupy the seats of their choice aboard public transportation, and that state law specified:

"*Should any passenger refuse to occupy the compartment . . . to which he is assigned by the officer or employee of such motor vehicle or bus company . . . said agent or employee shall have the power . . . to eject such person from such room, and for which neither they nor the motor vehicle or bus company which they represent shall be liable for damage in any of the courts of this state.*"

Although seldom enforced anymore outside the Deep South (many have been voided by federal legislation and court action and remain only as relics), state and local laws governing Negroes, Indians and other minorities have remained ghastly testimonies of the failure of America's democratic experiment. Following is a round-up of some of the more bizarre laws still on statute books across the country:

LOUISIANA: "*All street railway companies carrying passengers in their cars in this state shall provide equal but separate accommodations for the white and colored races by providing two or more cars or by dividing their cars by wooden or wire screen partitions . . .*"

ARKANSAS: "Separate bunks, beds, bedding, separate dining tables and all other furnishings, shall be provided and kept . . . for the use of white and negro prisoners, and it shall be unlawful for [such facilities] . . . after having been used by white or negro prisoners, to be changed the one for the use of the other."

KENTUCKY: "*Any person who presents or participates in the presentation of, or permits to be presented in any theater or other building under his control, any play that is based upon antagonism between master and slave . . . shall be fined not less than one hundred ($100) dollars, or imprisoned for not less than one nor more than three months, or both.*"

GEORGIA: "Any charge or intimation against a white female of having sexual intercourse with a person of color is slanderous without proof of special damage."

MISSISSIPPI: *"Any person, firm or corporation who shall be guilty of printing, publishing or circulating printed, typewritten or written matter urging or presenting for public acceptance or general information, arguments or suggestions in favor of social equality or of intermarriage between whites and negroes, shall be guilty of a misdemeanor and subject to a fine not exceeding five hundred ($500.00) dollars or imprisonment not exceeding six (6) months or both fine and imprisonment in the discretion of the court."*

KENTUCKY: "No textbook issued . . . to a white school child shall ever be re-issued to a colored school child, and no textbook issued to a colored school child shall ever be re-issued to a white school child."

VIRGINIA: *"The wilfull making of a (racially) false registration or birth certificate shall be punished by confinement in the penitentiary for one (1) year."*

VIRGINIA: "If the passenger fails to disclose his race, the (train) conductor . . . acting in good faith, shall be the sole judge of his race . . ."

ALABAMA: *"There shall be proper separation [in hospitals for the tubercular] of convicts from free persons, whites from blacks, males from females . . . The department [of Corrections and Institutions] shall be given general authority over the reception, care and segregation of such persons."*

SOUTH CAROLINA: "It shall be unlawful for any part, relative or other white person in this state . . . to dispose of, give or surrender [a] white child permanently into the custody . . . of a negro."

TENNESSEE: *"There are separate buildings on the grounds of hospitals for the insane for the colored insane in which they shall be kept."*

SOUTH CAROLINA: "No license shall be issued to any person of the white Caucasian race to operate a billiard room to be used by, frequented or patronized by, persons of the negro race; or to any person of the negro race to operate a billiard room to be used by, frequented or patronized by persons of the white or Caucasian race."

GEORGIA: *"The term 'white person' shall include only persons of the white or Caucasian race, who have no ascertainable trace of either Negro, African, West Indian, Asiatic Indian, Mongoloid, Japanese or Chinese blood in their veins. No person, any one of whose ancestors had been duly registered with the State Bureau of Vital Statistics as a colored person or person of color, shall be deemed to be a white person."*

ALLAN MORRISON

The White Power Structure

Since the Negro revolt ignited the fire that had been smolder-
ing for generations and shook America out of its complacency
about the racial problem, a key phrase, uttered by many of its
leaders as well as rank and file shock troops, has echoed
around the land: the White Power Structure. Seldom defined,
the term has become a vital part of the lexicon of the civil
rights movement, and a convenient synonym for the vast
complex of governmental authority, economic power and
military leadership which runs our society and maintains the
status quo against which the Negro is rebelling. This complicated structure of authority is the target of the Negro protest
movement's most vocal and militant spokesmen. The phrase is
not heard from the lips of the more moderate Negro leaders
like the NAACP's Roy Wilkins or the National Urban
League's Whitney Young, but to the younger Negro militants, whose economic philosophy veers left of center, it has
become both a watchword and a rallying cry.

The Negro freedom movement is understandably frag-
mented, and its leaders and component groups differ as to
ideology, tactics, timing and priorities, but all agree that they
face a common enemy, an impersonal hierarchy which pos-

sesses the power to keep Negroes in a pathological condition. But it is not always clear to those who are involved in the civil rights struggle who precisely are the people who make up the power structure which governs the country economically, politically and militarily. There is a general vagueness in "the movement" about the identities of the men who occupy the pivotal positions from which they can make major decisions affecting the destinies of millions.

To succeed, a revolution's leadership must understand the nature of its adversary and decide how best to deal with him. The Negro protest movement, emerging from its protest stage, is learning more about its opposition and how it operates. Like the labor upsurge of the 30s, the Negro movement has had to do its homework and discover who occupies the command posts of our economy and society. In its struggles with monopolies in the basic industries, the CIO hired trained economists to whom facts were weapons. Economic and scientific political research is no less essential to today's civil rights fighters.

Every important revolution in history has been conducted against an identifiable and visible enemy—a class or a nation— from which it sought either basic reforms, partial surrender of power or total abdication. The French Revolution was an uprising against a feudal aristocracy blocking the way of a new dynamic bourgeoisie struggling for power. England's industrial revolution broke the political power of the landed aristocracy and made possible the growth of capitalism in that country. The American Revolution crushed a colonial system. The Russian Revolution wiped out czarism and a society ruled by a feudal nobility.

The Negro revolt of the 60s is being fought for such recognizable goals as equality, justice, full opportunity to develop and enjoy citizenship and an end to the humiliation of segregation which breeds inferiority. This is a unique revolt which does not seek an end to the existing society or the destruction of its rulers. The Negro's leaders repeatedly declare that the revolt is not aimed at the 173 million whites who make up the predominant group, but against a relatively small but rarely identified power structure composed of people who really run the country and from whom it seeks to wrest fundamental concessions and reforms either through persuasion or direct action.

America's power structure, consisting of the highest influence-wielding economic, political and military circles, probably numbers no more than 5,000 persons. They are the same forces against whom the nation's labor movement and liberals find themselves arrayed on many policy questions. To Negroes, this powerful elite group has another important dimension: color. For those who run the country's biggest corporations, control the machinery of state and direct the military establishment are white. "There is a cultural and institutional tradition that white people exploit Negroes," said the eminent Swedish economist Gunnar Myrdal in his classic study of the U.S. race problem *An American Dilemma*. "Discrimination against Negroes is thus rooted in this tradition of economic exploitation."

Though the central enemy is recognized in a very loose sense as a white elite occupying the seats of power, the Negro movement for equality cannot present a unified national strategy against the men of power, some of whom are invisible and faceless. "We know that the white power structure exists," a CORE official stated, "but it is so scattered, so huge and so powerful that it is often difficult to mount an effective strategy against it." The civil rights movement makes its demands on the power structure and backs these up with demonstrations on the national, regional and local levels.

The 1963 March on Washington asserted the Negro's mood to the entire White Establishment including the Kennedy Administration. But after the pageantry and the speeches ended, the ten top March leaders conferred with the late President Kennedy, Chief Executive of the nation. The confrontation there was with the No. 1 symbol of government. The historic Selma-Montgomery march, though national in its impact, was essentially for Negro voting rights on the local level, and the marcher's chief antagonists were Sheriff James G. Clark of Selma and Alabama's notorious Governor George C. Wallace.

Clark represented the power structure of his county, fighting viciously to prevent Negroes there from participating in local government; while Wallace symbolized the state and Deep Southern regional power structures. From Washington to Bogalusa, La., the civil rights movement has been probing for the sensitive pressure points at which it must fight its battles against bigotry. But it must first know where the seats of real power are and who occupies them.

What, first of all, is power? Bertrand Russell once defined power as "the production of intended effects," giving power the quality of a property which can be owned by an individual or a group. "Power," wrote political scientist Harold D. Lasswell, "is participation in the making of decisions." The late English economist, Professor R. H. Tawney, a socialist by philosophy, said: "Power may be defined as the capacity of an individual or group of individuals, to modify the conduct of other individuals or groups in the manner which he desires."

The structure of power in America is centered in three major institutions, which by their centralized influence and the great consequences of the decisions which they make, shape great events and determine developments. These are the economy, the political system, and the military establishment. In all of these areas executive and administrative powers have increased in recent years to an awesome degree. The most powerful persons in the nation, therefore, are those who control these institutions. If this premise is accepted, then we must conclude that real power in the U.S. is concentrated in the hands of a few thousand individuals, headed by a power elite of political leaders and government officials, five-star generals and admirals, and the main owners and chief executives of the biggest industrial corporations.

Those who are members of the power structure blandly deny that they are powerful, while, outside it, numerous economists, political scientists and self-styled radical intellectuals reject the notion that such a group exists. But the U.S. power system is now clearly discernible. What used to be called "the invisible government" is now largely visible. A growing centralization of power in a narrowing circle of politicians, industrialists and military leaders has endowed the big decisions which they make with a greater significance than at any time in the history of man.

The core of America's power system is the highly concentrated group of men who own and manage big property. These are the corporate rich who include the chief executives of the top corporations. Who are the industrial overlords of the United States today? In the 1950s a comprehensive survey was made of the 900 top executives in U.S. industry culled from the nation's 250 largest industrial companies, 25 biggest railroads and 25 biggest utilities. Total yearly sales for the 300 top companies examined were $122 billion. Officers included in the study were either chairmen, presidents, executive vice presidents or plain vice presidents. The characteristics of this powerful group of industry executives are the same today: white, college-trained, hired in their 20s, served their corporations for 30 years, age between 50 and 60, and annual salaries in the $70,000-$80,000 range.

In the East, where economic and political power in the U.S. is concentrated, a white-Anglo-Saxon-Protestant establishment holds sway but its power and authority are diminishing and it is feeling the pressure to open its ranks to formerly excluded groups like the Jews.

Racial and religious prejudices are weakening the power of certain cricles of the financial and industrial power structure and threatening their continued control over the public. In a remarkable book, *The Protestant Establishment: Aristocracy and Caste in America*, E. Digby Baltzell writes: ". . . in order for an upper class to maintain a continuity of power and authority, especially in an opportunitarian and mobile society such as ours, its membership must, in the long run, be representative of the composition of society as a whole." The present power structure of the U.S. is clearly not representative of the population. There are no non-whites on either the national cabinet,* the U.S. Joint Chiefs of Staff, or the executive bodies of the National Association of Manufacturers, the U.S. Chamber of Commerce, the American Bankers Association or the National Industrial Conference Board.

Indications are that if American society is going to survive on its present bases, its leadership structure will have to be reorganized by the admission of groups traditionally excluded from it. Its future, if it has one, will rest on whether it can establish one valid principle of discrimination: on the basis of accomplishment and qualification rather than on ethnic or racial considerations.

Until the election in 1960 of John Fitzgerald Kennedy to the presidency, the U.S. political leadership elite was confined to the white-Anglo-Saxon-Protestant caste. Kennedy's breakthrough symbolized an ethnic-religious reorientation of the establishment on the power level which has not yet taken in the Negro. Jews are still victims of the cast line in the establishment as Negroes are of the color line. Jews constitute an

---

* Robert C. Weaver was appointed Secretary to the recently created Department of Housing and Urban Development in January, 1966, the first Negro to hold a cabinet post.

important and influential part of the leadership of American science, education, arts and business, but are generally excluded from the top circles of the power structure. An example: one in every seven graduates of the Harvard Business School is Jewish, but of the carefully selected trainees from business who return to Harvard for the Advanced Management Program only one in 200 is Jewish.

At the top of the pyramid of the U.S. economy about 150 people earn a million dollars or more a year, another 400 or so receive between $500,000 and a million. Some 1,500 persons earn from $250,000 to $500,000. These are the propertied since the income of two-thirds of the people in the $100,000–$1,000,000 bracket is derived from dividends, capital gains, estates or trusts. The thrust of the civil rights movement to desegregate the national housing market has very grave implications for most of these upper-income Americans.

High finance undergirds the power structure. A number of powerful oligarchies like the Rockefellers, Ford, General Motors, and the J. P. Morgan and DuPont interests have commanding positions. Ten years ago the Rockefeller family holdings were reported as $3,515 million, but the total assets of Rockefeller-controlled interests exceeded $61 billion. The DuPont family fortune in 1956 was estimated at $4,660 million in corporate assets, while the Mellon family interests totalled $3,769 million. All of the great American family fortunes, for better or worse, belong in the power structure picture. A handful of multimillionaire families, like the Rockefellers and Rosenwalds, have consistently given generous assistance to Negro education.

Certain sections of big business have made substantial contributions to Negro advance through the United Negro College Fund. Contributions from industry to Negro education have reached unprecedented levels since the civil rights drive began. "I attribute it to the growing recognition by the leaders of government and industry that the Negro people in the United States must now be brought to the level of full and effective citizenship," explains Dr. Frederick D. Patterson, president of the United Negro College Fund, which has raised $90 million since its founding in 1944, more than 75 per cent of which has come from business, industry and foundations.

Dispensing benefactions to the Negro is a tradition with a few wealthy white families which pre-dates the Civil War. The Rockefellers are a notable example. During slavery one Rockefeller aided fugitive slaves to escape via the legendary Underground Railroad. Today, New York's Governor Nelson Rockefeller entertains Martin Luther King Jr. as a private dinner guest at the State Mansion in Albany, N.Y.; John D. Rockefeller III is the earnest chairman of the national council of the United Negro College Fund; Rodman C. Rockefeller, son of Nelson, is co-chairman of the Interracial Council for Business Opportunity which seeks to encourage the growth of small Negro businesses; Winthrop Rockefeller has long been an active supporter of the National Urban League. But these are isolated examples of philanthropy and concern for human rights by individual members of one of the most powerful dynasties in American life and are by no means typical of their class.

"Many of the leaders of American business and industry now recognize that the Negro has to receive the same education as other American youth and has to have the same opportunities for employment and expression as other Americans, and that the failure to provide this is a drag on the national economy and a source of embarrassment to American leadership among the free peoples of the world," concludes Dr. Patterson. A capital development fund drive for $50 million launched by the United Negro College Fund in 1963 received large contributions from some of the leading units of the corporate power structure. The Ford Foundation gave $18 million, the Carnegie Corporation $2½ million, the Ford

Motor Company $500,000, the Kresge Foundation $500,000 and Standard Oil of N.J. $500,000. Such efforts by corporate wealth to raise Negroes' educational level are small but represent a kind of trend toward undoing the grievous damage done to the Negro by racial discrimination over many generations. Nowadays when big business helps the Negro it is not motivated necessarily by idealism but by self-interest.

The leaders of the National Urban League, the one Negro leadership organization which maintains steady contact with substantial elements of the white power structure, have no illusions about why U.S. businessmen and industrialists are slowly opening the doors of economic opportunity to Negroes. "The power structure," says Whitney Young Jr., executive director of the League, "is no longer a monolithic body of a few people who make the big decisions. Power is located in centers of influence. Power is in the labor movement as well as the civil rights movement. The major corporations of the country have belatedly but quite soundly decided that they must intervene in the civil rights struggle."

Within the last few years a small number of American corporations in the top bracket have authorized participation in the National Urban League's Commerce and Industry Council of 45 company executives, many of whom are included in the top 1,000 U.S. corporation officials belonging to the national economic power structure. "The leaders of industry are becoming more liberal and sensitive about the racial crisis mainly out of enlightened self-interest," remarks Whitney Young Jr. "They know that they can't sell the U.S. free enterprise system to foreign dark-skinned peoples when black people in America don't get their fair share of the rewards of the system."

The men who control the power and wealth of the higher corporate world have realized that business cannot function effectively and profitably on racial tension, conflict and violence. Such conditions are unhealthy for business. Racial boycotts of industrial concerns have greatly perturbed captains of industry.

The power structure in recent years has shown increasing anxiety that the wealthy state it operates might be threatened and damaged by such internal disorders as strikes, riots and racial outbreaks and protests. Beyond the fear of the destruction of its power, profits and interests by domestic convulsions, the power system is now obsessed by a fear that their entire society might be swept away in a nuclear war.

As in the economy, a small but wilful band of powerful men, numbering no more than 75, occupies the command posts of the executive branch of the federal government where high policy is made and executive decisions settled. This top circle of the country's governing apparatus consists of the president, vice-president, the cabinet, and the heads of the main government agencies, departments and commissions. Except for three Negroes—Robert C. Weaver, director of the Housing and Home Finance Agency, Carl Rowan, U.S.I.A. director, and Hobart Taylor, who is a special counsel with the President's executive staff—this hierarchy of government is a white club.* Few are professional politicians or have been trained in party politics. The White House staff and the cabinet represent the pinnacle of political power in America, but there is within Congress a special power structure of key decision makers.

All of the members of Congress, both the House of Representatives and the Senate, must be considered in the national political power system to a degree because they contribute to the making of legislative decisions which have national and international consequences, but only two of the six Negro members of the House of Representatives, Congressmen Adam Clayton Powell and William Dawson possess meaning-

---

* Robert C. Weaver appointed Secretary, Department of Housing and Urban Development, January, 1966; Carl Rowan, resigned U.S.I.A. directorship, 1965; Hobart Taylor appointed director, Import Export Bank, 1965.

ful power by virtue of being the chairmen of strategic congressional committees. Powell and Dawson, it should be noted, owe their membership in the power structure, not to the dominant white majority but to big-city constituencies which are practically all-Negro.

Since the 1880's the U.S. Senate has been an all-white body. No Negro has ever served in a federal cabinet, but if President Johnson decides to make Robert Weaver the first head of the proposed department of housing and urban development this lily-white tradition will have been broken. The cabinet is nominally the president's council of advisers, but its authority has declined in recent years. A powerful body, the seven member National Security Council now wields much of the power formerly held by the cabinet. A strategic planning agency located at the very apex of the governmental structure, the NSC is really the country's top board of directors for the nation's security. The Council's authority and scope are vast, and embrace military strategy, nuclear policy, economic aid and some domestic questions. The President relies on its membership for advice on crucial issues.

Enormous power to advise, plan and manage the nation's defenses and its offensive capabilities reside in the U.S. Joint Chiefs of Staff, a five-man council of military advisers to the President, the National Security Council and the secretary of defense. The Joint Chiefs of Staff do not make national policy but plan for war.

Labor is a definite factor in the American structure because it controls the organization of most of the national labor market, because its union treasuries contain hundreds of millions of dollars and because the Negro revolution has been forced to confront it squarely as a major institution responsible for the exclusion of black workers from skilled trades. Before the rise of the CIO in the 30s, U.S. labor presented the Negro with an agonizing dilemma: whether to oppose it along with the rest of the power structure, or join forces with it and work for racial reforms from inside. "There are really two power structures, one corporate and the other labor," observes A. Philip Randolph, sole Negro member of the A.F.L.-C.I.O. excutive council and now the elder statesman of the Negro rights movement. "The Negro has to decide which of these forces he wants to ally himself with. The labor power structure offers the greatest opportunity for economic advancement. First, labor is not free, and the Negro is not free. There is, therefore, a natural alliance between labor and the Negro. Neither labor nor the Negro has yet recognized this natural affinity."

Randolph notes that corporate power in the U.S. is white and will probably remain so. "I don't see any change coming soon in the racial composition of the power structure," he says pessimistically. "A few Negroes have been admitted to lower managerial positions in the structure, but real power is held by the whites. The power structure is all white because Negroes have never possessed investment capital in any quantity to enter it."

The Negro revolt moves into its next phase armed with the weapons of the strongest, most sweeping civil rights laws ever passed in history. A decisive period of implementation of this legislation has now opened up. To achieve their constitutional and human rights, Negroes will have to employ many tools and techniques. To complete the unfinished revolution, Negroes will make the transition from protest to planning for freedom, from propaganda to preparation to use widening opportunities. In the mid-1960s, the Negro revolt has learned a great deal about what the power structure is and who comprise it. The inclusion of seven Negroes in the top 5,000 of the higher circles is no measure of a pattern of integration but merely underlines the grim reality that the nation's power structure is 99.998 per cent white.

SIMEON BOOKER

The Great Society

The limousine headed through the White House gate on a
chilly December evening. President Lyndon B. Johnson had
not eaten dinner and his aides (two Negroes, Hobart Taylor
and Clifford Alexander, and one white, Lee C. White) had
strict orders to get him back to the White House within 45
minutes. Tired and not in the best humor, LBJ also had
another worry. An operation on his right hand (to remove
warts) left him only one, his left, to glad hand admirers and
friends. Within minutes the police-escorted vehicle arrived
at the Sheraton Park Hotel and LBJ appeared before the
Community Action Assembly of the National Urban League.

Some 300 representatives of groups, which League public
relations men boasted represented 10 million Negroes, suspi-
ciously awaited the nation's first Southerner elected President
in a half century. There was no enthusiastic welcome as LBJ
was introduced by Executive Director Whitney M. Young.

Surveying the crowd, the President started off in his Texan
drawl complimenting the League for its leadership in domestic affairs. Then he began to enumerate his lifetime goal,
stating:

"And until every qualified person, regardless of the house

where he worships . . . or the state where he resides . . . or the color of his skin . . . or the way he spells his name . . . until he has the right, unquestioned and unrestrained— to go in and cast his ballot in every precinct in this country, I am not going to be satisfied."

His hand upraised and his face grim, LBJ spotlighted the major civil rights goal of his forthcoming Great Society administration. There would be no compromise. There would be no retreat. The Chief Executive forthrightly committed himself to "the full assimilation of Negroes into American life," a bold and adventurous program which he felt no hesitancy to spell out.

This was the turning point. The reaction was tremendous. To a man and woman, the stunned Negro audience arose and vigorously applauded, cheering, hooting "bravo," and some women even cried. It was an emotional scene and even LBJ was touched by his evangelistic fervor.

Aides—acting under orders—clutched at the President's arm to hasten him from the stage and out of the room, but LBJ would not agree to a quick exit—even without dinner. He wanted personally to greet every one of the 300-odd participants—even with an injured and sore right hand. He was visibly touched, as were the listeners. En route to the White House 45 minutes over schedule, LBJ told his riders that he "would do something about Negro voting. I don't know," he said, "but I've got to do something."

Previously no President had appeared before a Negro audience prior to his inauguration. In politics, the six weeks between the November election and the January inauguration is satirically dubbed "the white folks hunting season" since white politicians rustle the best jobs and appointments in the new Administration during this time. Negroes are lucky to get a major post in the first six months.

The LBJ appearance before the middle-class Negro group demonstrated two points: 1) Negroes wanted no conservative, complacent Chief Executive, especially after they over-whelmingly voted for him against segregationist GOP Sen-ator Barry Goldwater, and 2) LBJ obviously intended to strike out in the tradition of a Westerner in charting new race relations trails. When he ran as the Vice Presidential nominee in 1960 on the ticket of the late John F. Kennedy, the Texan found liberals in some Northern communities removing the welcome mat and his intensive campaigning had to be done in the South and West. After the sudden death of JFK, when morale alarmingly dipped among Negroes, the veteran law-maker "wobbled" in finding the "correct Presidential pos-ture" to accommodate his former Southern colleagues who controlled Capitol Hill, the liberals, and the diverse Negro elements ranging from the historically legal-action oriented NAACP to the direct action groups such as SCLC, SNCC and CORE.

Overnight the longtime lawmaker was forced to formulate a bright political personality and a new program to capture the imagination of a majority of Americans.

One of the formidable landmarks of the first LBJ months was enactment of a broad civil rights law during the summer of 1964. Recommended by JFK, the bill was vigorously backed by LBJ in both the House and Senate and its passage produced the first evidence of the shape of the Great Society. Because of his legislative prowess, President Johnson was able to convert a bill into law, an idea into a program, and a word into action. His voice was molasses slow and raspy but he developed the knack early of being not only an effective speaker but a do-it-yourself President. Meeting with Negro leaders in an effort to maintain communications and respect their power positions, LBJ also used the job channel to develop additional popular support. He named Carl Rowan to the USIA directorship and even put Miss Gerri Whittington on his private secretarial staff at the White House.

But LBJ wanted no continuation of the JFK era. He

wanted his own show, his own program, his own people and he wanted his Administration to take roots and sprout into a period of progress and success. The era, which he dubbed "The Great Society," made its debut at his Inauguration.

From the time President Johnson delivered a moving Inaugural speech to his last visit to an Inaugural Ball, the purpose of the Great Society rang loud and clear. In a speech on Capitol Hill, the Chief spoke these unforgettable words: "Justice requires us to remember when any citizen denies his fellow citizen saying his color is not mine or his beliefs are different, in that moment he betrays America though his forebears created the nation." Throughout the inaugural program, the President lived up to the "assimilation" theme of his Administration. While integrated units marched past him in the Presidential box, the new Chief Executive beckoned Negro leaders to his side and was televised talking to them. Negro guests were scattered throughout the Presidential confines at every function, booked in every hotel and motel, and featured on every program, and invited in number to every event. An aide commented, "It's the President's wish." Defying age-old custom, LBJ in full view of 12,500 guests danced with Mrs. Hobart Taylor, whose husband is the White House counsel and the executive director of his Committee on Equal Opportunity in Employment. The incident publicized in the nation's press showed the affection and sincerity that pervaded the nation's capital as the era of the Great Society was ushered in.

A backlog of legislation in Congress was whittled down. New programs in anti-poverty, education, welfare, area redevelopment, anti-business recession, and medicare were proposed and fashioned. The transformation was so noticeable, Senator Paul Douglas (D., Ill.) wrote his constituents last April that, "Each year during the Easter recess of Congress, reporters in Washington take pen in hand and write that Congress has done nothing for four months. This year is different. Washington reporters are writing that no Congress in over 30 years has passed so much meaningful legislation in such a short time. This is true."

"The Great Society," said Louis Martin, deputy chairman of the Democratic National Committee, "will put the New Deal in the shade. LBJ provided tools for millions of Americans to improve themselves. Money has been allotted and programs fast are taking shape in a new bright period of progress. The Great Society starts from birth (Head Start) and goes to the grave (Senior Citizens). What counts now is whether Negroes will take full advantage of what is offered."

"It is the most dynamic program ever sponsored by an administration" Martin frequently has told gatherings about the country. "This is a program which will lift the floor of our middle class and the ceiling for thousands of deprived and disillusioned Negroes. It is the hope for Negroes in America."

Considered one of the most militant Negroes in the nation's capital, the NAACP's Clarence Mitchell viewed the Great Society as the crucial turning point in the Negro's struggle for civil rights. "I think the vote of Negroes for LBJ marked a breakthrough. The election overcame the handicap for Southern whites and Northern Negroes," Mitchell explained.

The only Negro lobbyist in Washington, Mitchell formerly refused to attend smoke-filled political parleys, inaugurations and social functions. Big, aggressive Mitchell changed his way of life for LBJ. He attended the first Inauguration in more than a quarter of a century and even participated in other functions as a LBJ guest. "The Great Society is an adequate blueprint for improving conditions for millions of Americans, black and white," Mitchell pointed out. "However, there is the gap between the President's wishes and the implementation of the program. How much and how far these projects will be carried out will determine the real value of the Great Society," he said.

The love and affection of the Negro Big Six leadership

force for LBJ is one of the most fantastic public relations achievements of the Great Society. Instead of the push and shove tactics of the past, Negro leaders now use a teamwork approach and actually help counsel LBJ on direction and even staffing of administration posts. As a result of the relationship, there is little Negro criticism of the Great Society—despite the obvious slowness in reaching into the big Negro communities with many of the programs. And ironically, many of the exponents—and opponents, too—of changes in civil rights techniques and approaches now are white.

This factor was demonstrated during the vote law push. When Alabama lawmen clubbed the first wave of Montgomery-bound voteless marchers on Bloody Sunday, a 1,000-plus clergy assembled in Washington and demanded that President Johnson immediately halt violence in the Dixie state. When a delegation from the body met with LBJ at the White House, the Chief Executive was shaken. The most vocal and militant of the ministers—even those criticizing him for being silent for almost a week—were white. The stand of the predominantly white clergymen from 35 states was unprecedented and unexpected and the indignation and growing clamor from whites, was a key factor in influencing LBJ's appearance days later on Capitol Hill to urge passage of a new and strong voting rights law—which his aides only a few months before said was not needed.

With applause ringing in his ears, President Johnson in a nationally televised speech urging immediate passage of a vote bill, declared: "There is no Negro problem. There is no Southern problem or Northern problem. There is only an American problem."

Then, almost outrightly backing the demonstrators, he challenged: "But even if we pass this bill, the battle will not be over. What happened in Selma is part of a far larger movement which reaches into every section and state of

America. It is the effort of American Negroes to secure for themselves the full blessings of American life."

In the words which converted his speech into the annals of political glory, LBJ later said: "Their cause must be our cause, too. It is not just Negroes, but all of us, who must overcome the crippling legacy of bigotry and injustice. *And we shall overcome.*"

The nocturnal Congressional message, widely hailed by civil rights leaders (several of whom were invited to sit in the presidential box to hear the delivery), became the keystone for action on the major Great Society target—which LBJ earlier set at a Negro meeting. The outrage of the whites solidified the determination. When the President told the ministers that his daughter couldn't sleep because of White House pickets singing, *We Shall Overcome*, one of the clerics retorted: "You shouldn't sleep either. You should be taking action to end this kind of violence." LBJ told Negroes he believed voting rights should be a cardinal goal and he used the build-up in indignation and fury to hop, step and jump to one of his most impressive ambitions—passage of the voting bill.

Running the Great Society with an iron fist, President Johnson has attracted few of the recognized liberals who years before proposed programs to reach the millions of America's disadvantaged. There are scarcely any functioning liberals left in the LBJ inner circle and even Negro leaders are beginning to sour on the liberal set—in accordance with LBJ's taste. One leader the other day said "the articulate liberals had the proposals but it took the President to carry them out with a combination of Confederates, Yankees, DAR and NAACP." LBJ flattened the liberal movement while at the same time the Great Society welcomed some of the most notorious race hate lawmakers on Capitol Hill. Expecting Negroes to accept these fellows is comparable to asking Jews to accept their former Nazi persecutors in a new government. But even more than this, LBJ aides have gone about attacking liberals and making it appear to our Negro middle class that liberals who sided with them for years are now their enemies while the newly shifted Southern politicians are our best friends. It is the follow-the-leader technique which has enthralled Negro intellectuals in Washington.

"Liberals can't produce," a topflight Negro official in government told a gathering. "They do all the talking about the world of tomorrow but they can't bring this world about. It took a President like LBJ to merge all of the factions, develop congressional support, and produce a Great Society. He has the secret. He has the tools, and he can do the job."

In such changing times, polls show LBJ maintaining white popularity even when shackled by his strong civil rights reputation. This is a worrisome question for the scattering liberal white set because there has been no great reform in civil rights from top to bottom in government or from agency to department or from Northern to Southern state. As usual, there is more talk, speeches and press notices than implementation and enforcement. The gains have been slow and difficult in government, but at least there have been gains—and symbolic gains. For the first time, perhaps, a Southern U.S. President clearly outlined what the purpose of a democracy should be and honestly tried to hammer out a program to fit the measurement. But no one man can radically change the course of U.S. race relations—not even a President. "This is a white man's country," you hear in Washington as well as in Montgomery, Alabama and you don't need to listen at a Klan meeting to understand.

Everywhere, white opposition has braked the desegregation speed of the Great Society program, and controlled its impact —even in the North. More acceptable at the cabinet and sub-cabinet level in Washington, where LBJ has a hand in operations, the Equal Opportunity committees aim to broaden the work base for the Negro. However, the farther you drop in grade and the farther you travel from the nation's capital, the more diluted you find the intent of the order and the program. Comprising a huge civil rights network with emphasis on percentages, gobbledegook and vast amounts of paper work, the race relations program is geared for the majority white with a message of love and tolerance and for the Negro to qualify for openings. Percentage-wise, the gains look good on paper. The number of Negroes in jobs above $10,000 has been so small that the addition of just one other person raises the percentage rating noticeably. However, numerically, the employment record is still far, far off course. With the thrust of the Great Society, EOP, FEP, LBJ, and the forces of government and industry are organized to lift the Negro into a better bargaining position. As the number of Negroes increases—from top to bottom—in all of the Great Society programs, there could be noticeable progress. At the present time, Negro gains are token and often the explanation from officials is that Negroes cannot qualify. Of nearly 1,000 U.S. generals, only one Negro, Benjamin O. Davis Jr. (son of the first token Negro general) can qualify and military reporters writing about him stress that he believes "race shouldn't be a factor in promotion." The few Negroes in government supergrade posts—with a top pay about $30,000-a-year—are now the highest paid Negro executives in the country, and the nation's capital is fast becoming the mecca for this new elite. But the white power structure has planted special restrictions on the Great Society stars. Before, it was joked that a Negro had to turn in his NAACP card and go through the ceremony of becoming a Negro white before he could be hired for a ranking federal post. Now whites are forcing the Negro government officials not only to disown the Negro militants but to move away from the Negro areas and leave their old cronies, to form a new buffer intellectual class in mixed neighborhoods.

To find integrated housing, however, is difficult. The most crucial sphere in race relations is housing and here the Great Society laid a goose egg. After naming a Negro, Dr. Robert C. Weaver, as U.S. housing administrator and appointing a presidential committee to enforce a badly contrived order, the gains have been so limited that not even members of the President's cabinet dare boast of Negro neighbors, so unpopular is the theme. Across the country, the weak housing order of the late JFK solidified opposition to mixed housing, incited financiers and builders to elude the integrationist dragnet and increase their profits by forcing gullible but prejudiced whites to pay more for houses because of added guarantees against the possibility of Negro neighbors.

In education, the Great Society promises hope for the illiterate and the poorly trained, vows to establish the pattern for building a new America from the rubble of city slums and Jim Crow public schools. In what direction and at what speed the administration heads can easily be the same way the LBJ cult moves in welfare, medicare and politics—gentle at first, then ruthlessly if there are constant barriers. When the anti-poverty legislation was first proposed in Congress, spokesmen didn't want Negroes to testify, for fear Southern white solons would get the impression Negroes would benefit too much from the pork barrel deal. Lawmakers slapped down an increase in welfare funds when it was discovered Negroes shared equally in some states. Southern governors revolted against a stern order of the education commissioner that public schools be desegregated within a few years and it was assumed the governors were pleased at the unpublicized compromise.

In essence, the Great Society is a political community with a vast program in blueprint stage in which the follow up or follow through depends upon the might of the white support or opposition. As a politician, LBJ reacts with sensitivity, understands resistance and pressures, and the more opposition churned up, the less forceful he might be if he becomes the under dog. His civil rights program—now so greatly condemned by conservative whites—could stop on dead center in the event the more liberal whites, now not a segment of the Society program, are not harnessed and brought into the fray. As one white government aide said: "LBJ had to win the presidency to favor civil rights. There is one President and 180 million white Americans who will not be President and can afford to be courageously prejudiced." This is the dilemma of Lyndon Baines Johnson and the dilemma of the Great Society.

At the Howard University June commencement, President Johnson in his fourth civil rights utterance admitted that Negroes "are trapped in inherited, gateless poverty." "They lack training and skills," explained LBJ to a 10,000-plus person audience of middle class (and trained) Negroes. "They are shut in slums, without decent medical care. Private and public poverty combine to cripple their capacities." Explaining more, LBJ charged that "It is the devastating heritage of long years of slavery and a century of oppression, hatred and injustice." Later, he emphasized that "there are differences—deep, corrosive, obstinate differences—radiating painful roots into the community, the family and the nature of the individual." After enlarging on the problem, LBJ announced an autumn conference at the White House to bring the best minds together for a discussion of new ways and remedies for the so called Negro problem.

The speech as did his three earlier major civil rights messages, electrified the Negro audience by its frankness and boldness. "Together and with millions more," LBJ told the robed graduates, "we can light that candle of understanding in the heart of America. And once lit, it will never go out."

What the President probably meant was that he was not

satisfied that the Great Society had solved the dilemma of the Negro in America. And perhaps, as he brought out, white America might show far more compassion and understanding in working out a successful remedial program than before. The future of his Great Society might very well be judged by the reaction of the majority white America—but never overlooking the tall, drawling Texan, who, once distrusted by Negroes as a Southerner, is well on his way to becoming a permanent figure in civil rights history.

ERA BELL THOMPSON

Some of My Best Friends
Are White

When Perle Mesta heard of Patricia Harris' appointment as ambassador to Luxembourg, she exclaimed: "I'm sure the people will like her. When I went to Luxembourg I took my butler and maid, who are colored, and the people adored them!"

I am just as sure that Perle Mesta, the "hostess with the mostest," diplomat and entrepreneur that she is, would not knowingly offend her colored successor to the Grand Duchy. But to equate the acceptance of America's first Negro woman envoy with that of an envoy's servants is the kind of *faux pas* that sends us liberal-minded Negroes running to the defense of some of our best friends, who happen to be white.

Lately, we have been doing a lot of running.

With the new order of things, the majority race is finding it difficult to alter a life-time of thinking of the Negro as an inferior and start treating him as an equal; to stop confining analogues to one race and start comparing merit with merit. Willie Mays is the highest paid baseball player in the major leagues, not the best "Negro player." Leontyne Price is a credit to the world of opera, not just "to her race." And between the butler and the ambassador, there are thousands of Negroes who will be tomorrow's neighbor, perhaps tomorrow's boss.

I was reared among white people and went to school with their children. My dearest playmate was a blue-eyed blonde. In the language of the Southland, I could say I had a "white mammy," for after my parents died I was taken into the home—and the hearts—of a white couple whom I still regard as my family. During this trying period of readjustment, we who know and understand white people should be tolerant and helpful. We must stand by while they emerge from the shock of finding that, shorn of his stereotypes, the Negro is a normal, living and breathing American. We must be alert so that they will not go overboard and envision every Negro as a paragon of virtue while suspecting every white man of being a cotton-picking bigot. We must protect them from taking disastrous liberties while caught up in the headiness of racial conversion and comfort them when they discover—and they will—that dark angels fall as well as fly.

The paternalistic attitude of master toward slave that ended with the civil war and reappeared as an urge to be patronizing toward the less fortunate of God's children, has upset more than one bilateral interracial relationship. In an effort to show their sincerity, my white friends are willing to give me the shirts off their backs, and some of them did, even though we worked on the same job, drew the same salary and had charge accounts at the same downtown stores. In an atmosphere of reproach, they have admired my automobile, then delivered a lengthy oration on why they drive a cheaper make or find it economically expedient to own no car at all.

This got so bad after I bought my first Buick that I tried to get a body and fender shop to turn it into a Chevy by plugging up the telltale vents. The same was true of a mouton coat I once owned. While new, it looked for all the world like beaver I could not afford. No matter how much I denied it, my white friends were sure that it was beaver until a sudden rainstorm turned the silky pelt into hard, kinky knots. Ironically, when I worked up to mink, my colored friends were just as sure that the fur was imitation.

While bemoaning our immaturity in things material, white people too often expect us—all of us—to be authorities on all matters pertaining to race. Yesterday every Negro co-worker, porter and committee member was being asked: "Aren't your people pushing too hard?" "Is Africa really ready for independence?" And with a hint of incrimination: "Isn't it awful what is happening in the Congo?" Today they want to know what we "think about the Black Muslims," and haven't our demonstrations "gone too far?"

Well, Africa is independent and what the Congolese did and are doing to anybody is deplorable and child's play compared with what Belgians did to the Congolese under the bloody reign of King Leopold II. Why bring up the Muslims? We don't go around asking our white friends to explain the Ku Klux Klan. To begin a conversation on the premise that the Negro is wrong in his urgency to gain full equality is more apt to start an argument than to inspire brotherhood. And if it is going to be that kind of party, let the nonwhite guest enjoy his martini before settling down to the inevitable seminar on "the problem." If his is a neophyte audience, make it a double scotch and go light on the questions. Being black does not make all of us jazz buffs and sports enthusiasts, nor does it give us a speaking acquaintance with the 22 million other Negroes in these United States.

Sensitive, yes. We Negroes are that, for every day in so many little ways we are reminded of our race. There are white people who greet me warmly in the privacy of their homes but turn formal when we meet in public. One white woman closed the blinds before she seated me in her living room and it was broad daylight. Another tells me that she would like to invite me over for dinner but is afraid her neighbors will object.

Recently *Ebony*'s promotion department sent out a number of letters to potential subscribers. Back came angry replies from several white people who had not yet fled from changing neighborhoods. One frantic woman put in a long distance call.

"Stop sending me your nigger literature!" she screamed. "Don't you know that I'm white?"

"We didn't know," she was told. "But as long as white people send us their literature, we will continue to send white people ours."

Being careful *not* to offend us can also be carried to ridiculous ends. A civic meeting held in a small Midwestern town was attended by a lone Negro woman. In the middle of a sentence, one of the ladies put a hand over her mouth and bolted from the room. Thinking she had suddenly taken ill, the Negro woman forgot the incident until the next day when she received a phone call.

"I want to apologize for my thoughtlessness," said the voice at the other end of the wire. "I just forgot you were there."

Mystified, the Negro woman asked what she had said. "Those dear little children in that housing project," she wailed. "I called them underprivileged!"

White people with a guilt complex feel compelled to continually remind themselves, as well as their dark friends, that they haven't a prejudiced bone in their bodies. To prove it, they love all Negroes, blindly join with or contribute to anything connected with his "cause." To them every colored tot is "cute" no matter how unkempt or illmannered it may be. The ordinary-looking brown girl behind the counter is "so attractive." The tan young man of average intelligence who works in the accounting department is "positively brilliant." Even those Negroes in whom these people can find no virtue, they defend with excuses.

Any clean-cut Negro, dark but not too dark; smart but not too forward, is a prince of a fellow and a prize to exhibit at sophisticated affairs. His presence is a status symbol. His quotes on race are proudly credited to "my good colored friend." Complains one prominent Negro professional: "Since the white people discovered me, I never get a minute's rest. Every week my wife and I are invited to their homes. It's gotten so bad that I just have to say no, to remind them that I have colored friends too."

In the business world there are inside jokes that are told only among members of the trade or business family. What Macy says to Gimbel is not repeated by Lord and Taylor. So it is with pet names and homely expressions Negroes toss around among themselves. They may be overheard by white friends, but used by them never. Occasionally one may be so completely identified with Negroes that his race is forgotten, but even he approaches the inside joke cautiously. Those who mistake the liberty of friendship for a license to repeat racial designations, even in jest, are courting disaster.

Disc jockey Marty Fay can scream, "Man! You ready for that!" Al Hirt can march his musical "Saints" down a night-club aisle and LBJ can tell a nation-wide television audience that "we shall overcome," but the first hint of dialect, the mention of a switchblade and comedy turns to drama.

We Negroes welcome the white man as a partner, but we do not want him taking over our fight. As in all lasting friendships, there is a line of propriety over which neither side must cross. Picket with us in Chicago, walk with us to Montgomery, but don't tell us where to start. Don't tell us when to stop. Give us credit for knowing where we want to go. And do not expect applause for every unselfish gesture. We are too busy worrying about how far we have yet to go to attain our goal to be cheered by how far we have come. Fighting against racial odds is an old, old story. We have been at it too long to get excited over a dislodged pebble while wrestling to remove the stones.

Going the full cycle, some of my white friends pass their probationary period with flying colors, fall in love with the excitement surrounding the civil rights movement, then retire to the sidelines and criticize. "What are you doing to help yourselves," they ask. And in the same breath: "You have made your point, why don't you get off the streets and let the courts take over?"

When white people become that confused, it makes me sad.

They march with us toward equality. They sing with us about freedom. They believe, like us, in the brotherhood of man, but some white people, even some of my best friends, are not ready for open occupancy. After all we have taught them about togetherness, they still think that we Negroes are happier with our own kind. One God, yes, in a split-level heaven: a side for Perle and a side for Pat.

Deep down in their hearts they know that's not right.

What Whites Can Learn
from Negroes

Trouble don't last always, says an old Negro spiritual, but according to screaming newspaper headlines, convulsed TV commentators and a frayed-nerved public, Old Man Trouble has pitched his teepee square in the middle of the twentieth century and settled down for a record run.

The whole world is on edge. Nations are bickering with nations. Races are pitted against races. Everybody seems beset by fears, overwrought by frustrations. They are jittery about the war in Viet Nam that had no beginning and the war that has no ending in the Dominican Republic and the cold war that occasionally gets mighty warm. They are hearing noises that do not exist, seeing objects that are not there.

In times like these, white people seeking a panacea for their problems might well take a lesson from the Negro on how to live in a troubled world. The Negro is an expert. He has known nothing but trouble all of his life. His grievances are multiple for he has all of the white man's fears and doubts plus the additional burden of being black. Yet the Negro can still smile, for the progress that he has made up from slavery to his present status—short of first class citizenship though it is—is one of the most remarkable advancements in the history of mankind. In the process he has learned to turn his liabilities into assets, to adjust to that over which he has no control and to have faith in his ability to overcome all of the other obstacles between himself and full equality.

The Philosophy of "If"

The way to tell a Negro from a white man when physical appearances failed, swore the old time armchair anthropologists, was to engage the suspect in conversation. Query him about his ambitions, his future plans, his next step. If he said he "hoped" to become a lawyer or a merchant, that he "wanted" to buy a car, spend his vacation in Canada, then that man was white. But if he prefaced his desire by the phrase: "If I live and nothing happens," he was colored. This homely philosophy with the built-in disaster clause allowed the Negro to take his setbacks and misfortunes in stride. It was this philosophy, born of heart-breaking experiences, which kept his insanity and suicide rates below those of his fair-skinned brothers. But today's Negro has added a positive dimension to a probable clause. If he lives, he will *make* something happen.

The white man stakes his all on a business venture or a political campaign. He will even put his life's savings in schemes that can pay off only with a hoped-for boom, and bet his last five dollars on a long-shot nag. If he loses he will have an opportunity to recoup and start all over again, but all too often, he is found below an open window or his last will and testament is contained in a brief note on the railing of a bridge.

The Negro, whose existence is riddled with reverses and disappointments, has learned not to put all of his eggs in one

shopping bag or his complete trust in one man. He knows that
if he fails, there is no second chance. For him there are no
short cuts to succcess. Only through his own supreme efforts
can he attain his cherished goal. When bad luck overtook
him, he used to console himself with the adage that "everything happens for the best." Today, he does not wait for
things to happen, and the best may not be good enough.
Instead of taking his troubles to the window or the water, he
is more likely to try them in the courts or dramatize them in
the streets.

The Negro is particularly adept at making the best of a bad
situation, not because of any inherent powers that he may
have, but because he has had an abundance of practice and
more bad situations than the white man. More put upon and
less protected than any other ethnic group in our society
except the Indian, he has been under the strain of racial
tensions all of his life; has always been handicapped by patterns of prejudice and walls of discrimination. The Negro in
America is kept so busy trying to live under the same flag as
the Ku Klux Klan, the White Citizens Councils and other
hate-Negro, hate-minority organizations, that he has little
time to worry about communism in China or India's population explosion.

A nuclear bomb which he may never see is not nearly as
imminent as an electric cattle prod he has felt. Wars in distant
lands in which he too must fight, are not as personal as
demonstrations in Chicago or boycotts in Birmingham. Although some white citizens would rather cloud the image of
this country abroad than practice democracy here at home,
the Negro remains loyal to America. He fights for it and he
dies for it and he hopes fervently that it will soon be at peace,
for he needs all his war-spent energies to earn his daily bread
and a little butter. Now that his right to the ballot has been
reaffirmed, he needs his war-spent strength to make things

happen: to lead registration drives in the South and to dis-
courage voter apathy in the North, to exercise his right to live
where his money and desires dictate, to obtain better education for his children, to fit himself for a better job so that he
can improve his standard of living. He knows that these
things are now possible, but wishing alone will not make
them so.

In the South and to some extent in the North, the Negro's
very existence once depended upon his ability to get along
with white people. The psychology of fear employed by race
supremacists to frighten him into 100 years of submission is
no longer applicable. His is the faith that overcomes, the
courage that marches around bigots and laughs at the Klan.
His is an example of faith and courage that other men might
follow.

Trapped in a white-dominated world, the black man has
learned to live with trouble. To yesterday's motto "don't get
mad, get smart," he has added "do something!" If white men
are to have peace of mind they must also stop getting mad and
getting nervous and do something. For one thing, they must
learn to live with men who are black and red and yellow and
brown. They, too, must learn to become bedfellows with fear
and frustration, to turn liabilities into assets, adjust to that
which cannot be helped and change those things that are
morally wrong.

To master the art of doing with and doing without is
essential to all men. With very little of this world's goods the
Negro has been able to an unbelievable degree to survive—
even thrive—under oppressions, uncertainties and inconven-
iences. He has worn hand-me-down clothing, lived in second
class housing, worked at low-paying jobs. But those conditions were morally wrong and he found a way to change
them. In doing so, he has transferred his disappointments into
hopes and hopes into actions and actions into improvements

which, if continued, will bring him the full equality and ultimate happiness all men seek.

If white people would profit by the Negro's ability to overcome, they can begin by cultivating his sense of humor. His public posture may be that of the angry young man, but his capacity to laugh at his troubles, even though he does so in the privacy of his race, is his means of releasing pent-up emotions. White people who would have peace of mind, must ease their guilty consciences. Like the Negro, they must put their trust in God and their shoulder to the wheel. Faith alone will not move mountains.

If the black man can make it by adding new dimensions to old adages, surely white men can follow his example. No people can have peace always nor can their prosperity continue unbroken. All of this country's citizens have worked hard and sacrificed much to make America the great nation that it is today. Surely those who by virtue of color have inherited the bulk of her many benefits can, like the Negro, learn to endure her limitations.

JOHN O. KILLENS

Black Man's Burden*

The "Negro Problem" and the "White Man's Burden" are
historical misnomers—logical inversions. The Problem never
was "Negro." The Problem is, and ever was, Caucasian—
Anglo-Saxon—European—white. And now, today, this very
moment, the problem facing most of the races of mankind is:
"What are we going to do about these Europeans? How are
we going to get them off our backs, and how are we going to
undo the centuries of deliberate dehumanization? And having
liberated ourselves from them, politically, economically, socially, psychologically, culturally, how are we going to inte-
grate them into the New World of Humanity, where racial
prejudice will be obsolete, where the whiteness of their skin
will not be held against them, but at the same time, will not
afford them any special privileges? How are we going to
teach them the meaning of some of the terms they themselves
claim to have invented, but never practiced, as far as we were
concerned; such terms as, "democracy," "human dignity,"
and the "brotherhood of man"? This is the enormous black
man's burden today. There never was a white man's burden,

* Copyright © 1965 by John Oliver Killens from the book *Black Man's
Burden* by John Oliver Killens. Reprinted by permission of Trident Press.

in this context, unless it was his guilty conscience, assuming that he had a conscience, where black men were concerned.

The Black Man's Burden was, simply stated, slavery and colonialism.

Once upon a time, not too many centuries ago, in time and space, men-of-little-pigmentation, who dwelt in the midget-sized countries of Europe, embarked on a bloody venture of empire. American aborigines dubbed these people, "pale-faces," a designation far more accurate than the one they chose for themselves. They preferred to look upon themselves as "white men." The "Pale-Faces" came from many and various tribes, who, not very long before, had lived in holes in the earth and had waged internecine wars and had worn no clothes save the skin of an animal which was thrown over the shoulders, and fastened at the breast by a thorn or a sharp pointed stick. A few centuries later, this palefaced barbaric people had become the "Master Race."

One of the most important things the Pale-Faced Ones did in those times was to discover America. A man named Christopher Columbus got the credit for it. Now obviously Columbus did not discover America, since there were people there when he arrived. The kindest thing you can say for old Christopher is: "He stumbled upon the place and cased the joint for Isabella." It was the same the whole world over. You did not exist until the great Pale-Faced Ones discovered you. You just waited in a kind of limbo. You just stood on some exotic piece of real estate in that vast continuing "jungle" that stretched from America to Africa to Asia to the islands of the mighty oceans, and, you "noble savage" you, you just waited to be "discovered," to be "civilized" and "Christianized," or annihilated. You had no alternatives.

Having "discovered" America, the Pale-Faced Ones stole black men from the continent of Africa and dubbed them "niggers" and brought them across the Atlantic Ocean in the holds of ships, stacked together like cordwood, men, women and children. Thousands of African villages were depopulated. Some still are to this very day. There is no problem of population explosion on that great continent. Peaceful villages were devastated. Chiefs and kings were corrupted, and many of the indigenes, who worked hand in glove with the "nigger catchers," were in their own turn made captives . . .

More than sixty million people lost their lives on the high seas, known those days as the Middle Passage. Most of the ships were death traps, floating plagues and epidemics. Wherever you were stacked at the beginning of the voyage, was where you spent the entire trip. You ate, you moved your bowels, you vomited, you urinated, you lived and slept in your own defecation. You got sick and you died all in your allotted spot. In the last stages of this lucrative trade, if you were one of the lucky ones, and a British ship spotted your outlaw ship on the high seas, your captain would throw the whole load of you overboard, chained to one another, and you would be spared the slow death of the ocean voyage and the even slower death that awaited you at the journey's end.

Most of the unfortunate survivors of the trip were sold into slavery in America, that haven for all men who cherished freedom. And thus evolved the cruelest irony in history. The Sweet Land of Liberty, the brave New World, this New Hope for mankind, became the stage upon which was enacted the most inhuman story in the entire history of man's brutality to man. By comparison with American slavery and the slave trade, the era of the Nazi bestiality was an exercise in tiddlywinks. The prime reasons the civilized world (meaning those who had fire power) did not rise up in protest, was that the victims were of a "pagan" and a "savage" race of people, and were indeed lucky to be brought to America under whatever conditions, to be "civilized" and "Christianized." But the blacks did not believe in their good fortune. Many leapt into the sea en masse; many others mutinied; every kind of method of committing suicide was attempted. The blacks were truly an ungrateful lot.

Having invented the Negro, to justify slavery, the Negro Invention was used as an apologia for the colonialization of three-quarters of the world's people. Asia and Africa and the Islands became the objects and the victims of these civilizing missions. Thus there evolved two kinds of people on this earth, men and non-men, white folks and "niggers," Christians and heathens, masters and slaves. On the one hand was the Master Race, on the other hand the Chosen People. From one-quarter of the earth's populations came the Men and the exploiters. They came from the Master Race—naturally. The rest of humanity were the Chosen People, chosen for exploitation and to live out their lives as non-humans. It is a peculiar thing the way Western man evinced such great shock at Der Führer's theory of the Master Race, when, for centuries, men of the West had taken this theory for granted in relation to the darker races who were the great majority of the people of the world.

But now we live at a moment when time is catching up with history. Throughout most of the earth, Time and History have entered into a conspiracy to put an end to the domination of the Pale Faced Ones, to bring the bottom to the top, to make the prophecy of the Elders come true; to wit, that "the stone the builders rejected shall become the head of the corner."

For our purpose in this dialogue, we will arbitrarily define the West as all of Europe, which means to us Europe, Canada, the U.S.A., New Zealand and Australia. And the Republic of South Africa. When we speak of the West, we mean the western and eastern part of Western civilization. The Cold War division of the world into Eastern and Western camps is but another example of the exaggerated self-importance with which the European looks upon himself. What he really means is Eastern and Western white people, and he demands that the rest of humanity joins one camp or the other. "You're either with me or against me!" both camps proclaim self-righteously.

But now, the people of this nation must make a grave decision. "To be or not to be." Whether to die along with the rest of the aging West, or to live in freedom and in dignity with the New World of the colored peoples. Put the question another way: "Is America too young to die of old age?"

Australia has to answer similar questions. "Are we Australians ready to live in equality with the races of mankind? Can we forego the prerogatives that historically accrued to the very fact of our whiteness?" There is Australia, a vast continent with a smaller population than the City of New York, instead of reaching out her hands to most of mankind residing on her doorsteps, she stares ten thousand miles away toward white men in the dying Western World. The two-thirds of humanity in her front yard are invisible to her. It seems to me that young Israel must also wipe the West out of her eyes and turn them toward the New World, which she must be a part of if she is to live and freely prosper, the New World which is neither East nor West, as we understand those Cold War terms, but somewhere in between where the twain is meeting, Rudyard Kipling notwithstanding.

At a time when a revolutionary and creative spirit was raging in the West, it gave the world great human values, such as the Common Law and habeas corpus, but the lid was clamped down on this spirit a long, long time ago. In the true context of time and space, this spirit died a-borning. And now in the middle of this century, the West is jaded, disillusioned, cynical. What more convincing evidence of the decadence of the West than the fact that they have now succeeded in achieving the means of mankind's total destruction? Eureka! It is the disgrace of the Western World that people are starving throughout the world; young folks in the bloom of life are dying of cancer and other "incurable" diseases, while governments of super-affluent nations spend billions on destruction and men in space and moon trips, and all in the name of progressive civilization. This is an obvious perversion of human energies and values. The hope of all humanity is for the New World to give mankind a new dialogue—a brand new set of values.

One has only to look at the map of the world as it was in 1945, and then compare it with the map as it is today, to get some idea of the decline of Western power and influence. There was a time just two decades ago when Englishmen could rightfully boast that the sun never set on the British Empire. It was the same time when France ruled great hunks of Africa and Asia. Colored peoples throughout the world were dominated by the pale-faced men of that medium-sized continent called Europe. Sir Winston Churchill must have had prescience of the future already becoming the present, when he proclaimed, with forced bravado, that he had not taken over the reins of Her Majesty's government to preside over the dissolvement of the British Empire.

That this civilization is at death's door, some Western sages will admit, and this is disquieting enough. But the suspicion, indeed the growing evidence, that the rest of the world will not voluntarily lie down and die along with the West is nothing short of terrifying to most of the Western wise men. And there is the rub; that the deadly germ killing the West is not irresistible, that three-quarters of the earth's people will fight off the germ, Genet and his avant-garde notwithstanding; that black and brown men will survive and write the West's obituary. Can you imagine the slave master living with the fear that his liberated slave will preach his, the master's funeral? Western man lives with a built-in nightmare that the disinherited will soon and finally inherit the earth and rewrite the history of the last five hundred years, and that "niggers" everywhere will be vindicated, from Birmingham to Johannesburg, which means that mankind, no matter the color, will at long last be vindicated.

Alain Albert was right when he said (in *Presence Africaine*) that one of the cruelest things Western man had done was to "build a fence between man and man." It should be obvious that Western man meant to fence three-quarters of mankind out, but what he has succeeded notably in doing, is to fence himself in. And so in the middle of the Twentieth Century, the West finds itself in a self-constructed isolation ward. The hope of America, indeed its sole salvation, is that the Freedom Movement will tear the fences down and bring this country into the family of mankind. This is a part of the black man's burden. But instead of tearing the fences down, the West seeks to extend the fences to enclose the entire world. At this late date, it wants everyone within the Pale.

JAMES BALDWIN

Unnameable Objects,
Unspeakable Crimes*

I have often wondered, and it is not a pleasant wonder, just
what white Americans talk about with one another. I wonder
this because they do not, after all, seem to find very much to
say to *me*, and I concluded long ago that they found the color
of my skin inhibitory. This color seems to operate as a most
disagreeable mirror, and a great deal of one's energy is ex-
pended in reassuring white Americans that they do not see
what *they* see. This is utterly futile, of course, since *they do*
see what *they* see. And what they see is an appallingly
oppressive and bloody history, known all over the world.
What they see is a disastrous, continuing, present, condition
which menaces them, and for which they bear an inescapable
responsibility. But since, in the main, they appear to lack the
energy to change this condition, they would rather not be
reminded of it. Does this mean that, in their conversations
with one another, they merely make reassuring sounds? It
scarcely seems possible, and yet, on the other hand, it seems all
too likely.

Whatever they bring to one another, it is certainly not
freedom from guilt.

* First printed under the title "White Man's Guilt."

173

The guilt remains, more deeply rooted, more securely lodged, than the oldest of old trees; and it can be unutterably exhausting to deal with people who, with a really dazzling ingenuity, a tireless agility, are perpetually defending themselves against charges which one has not made.

One does not have to make them. The record is there for all to read. It resounds all over the world. It might as well be written in the sky.

One wishes that Americans, white Americans, would read, for their own sakes, this record, and stop defending themselves against it. Only then will they be enabled to change their lives. The fact that Americans, white Americans, have not yet been able to do this—to face their history, to change their lives—hideously menaces this country. Indeed, it menaces the entire world.

For history, as nearly no one seems to know, is not merely something to be read. And it does not refer merely, or even principally, to the past. On the contrary, the great force of history comes from the fact that we carry it within us, are unconsciously controlled by it in many ways, and history is literally *present* in all that we do. It could scarcely be otherwise, since it is to history that we owe our frames of reference, our identities, and our aspirations.

And it is with great pain and terror that one begins to realize this. In great pain and terror, one begins to assess the history which has placed one where one is, and formed one's point of view. In great pain and terror, because, thereafter, one enters into battle with that historical creation, oneself, and attempts to re-create oneself according to a principle more humane and more liberating; one begins the attempt to achieve a level of personal maturity and freedom which robs history of its tyrannical power, and also changes history.

But, obviously, I am speaking as an historical creation which has had bitterly to contest its history, to wrestle with it and finally accept it, in order to bring myself out of it. My point of view is certainly formed by my history and it is probable that only a creature despised by history finds history a questionable matter. On the other hand, people who imagine that history flatters them (as it does, indeed, since they wrote it) are impaled on their history like a butterfly on a pin and become incapable of seeing or changing themselves or the world.

This is the place in which, it seems to me, most white Americans find themselves. They are dimly, or vividly, aware that the history they have fed themselves is mainly a lie, but they do not know how to release themselves from it, and they suffer enormously from the resulting personal incoherence. This incoherence is heard nowhere more plainly than in those stammering, terrified dialogues white Americans sometimes entertain with that black conscience, the black man in America.

The nature of this stammering can be reduced to a plea: Do not blame *me*. I was not there. I did not do it. My history has nothing to do with Europe or the slave trade. Anyway, it was *your* chiefs who sold *you* to *me*. I was not present on the middle passage. I am not responsible for the textile mills of Manchester, or the cotton fields of Mississippi. Besides, consider how the English, too, suffered in those mills and in those awful cities! I, also, despise the governors of Southern states and the sheriffs of Southern counties; and I also want your child to have a decent education and rise as high as his capabilities will permit. I have nothing against you, *nothing!* What have *you* got against *me*? *What do you want?*

But, on the same day, in another gathering, and in the most private chamber of his heart always, he, the white man, remains proud of that history for which he does not wish to pay, and from which, materially, he has profited so much. On that same day, in another gathering, and in the most private chamber of the black man's heart always, he finds himself facing the terrible roster of the lost: the dead, black junkie; the defeated, black father; the unutterably weary, black mother; the unutterably ruined black girl. And one begins to suspect an awful thing: that people believe that they *deserve* their history and that when they operate on this belief, they perish. But they can scarcely avoid believing that they deserve it—one's short time on this earth is very mysterious and very dark and hard. I have known many black men and women and black boys and girls, who really believed that it was better to be white than black, whose lives were ruined or ended by this belief; and I myself carried the seeds of this destruction within me for a long time.

Now, if I, as a black man, profoundly believe that I deserve my history and deserve to be treated as I am, then I must also, fatally, believe that white people deserve their history and deserve the power and the glory which their testimony and the evidence of my own senses assure me that they have. And if black people fall into this trap, the trap of believing that they deserve their fate, white people fall into the yet more stunning and intricate trap of believing that they deserve *their* fate, and their comparative safety; and that black people, therefore, need only do as white people have done to rise to where white people now are. But this simply cannot be said, not only for reasons of politeness or charity, but also because white people carry in them a carefully muffled fear that black people long to do to others what has been done to them. Moreover, the history of white people has led them to a fearful, baffling place where they have begun to lose touch with reality—to lose touch, that is, with themselves—and where they certainly are not happy. They do not know how this came about; they do not dare examine how this came about. On the one hand, they can scarcely dare to open a dialogue which must, if it is honest, become a personal confession—a cry for help and healing, which is really, I think, the basis of all dialogues—and, on the other hand, the black man can scarcely dare to open a dialogue which must, if it is honest, become a personal confession which, fatally, contains an accusation. And yet, if we cannot do this, each of us will perish in those traps in which we have been struggling for so long.

The American situation is very peculiar, and it may be without precedent in the world. No curtain under heaven is heavier than that curtain of guilt and lies behind which Americans hide: it may prove to be yet more deadly to the lives of human beings than that iron curtain of which we speak so much—and know so little. The American curtain is color. We have used this word, this concept, to justify unspeakable crimes, not only in the past, but in the present. One can measure very neatly the white American's distance from his conscience—from himself—by observing the distance between himself and black people. One has only to ask oneself who established this distance. Who is this distance designed to protect? And from what is this distance designed to protect him?

I have seen this very vividly, for example, in the eyes of Southern law enforcement officers barring, let us say, the door to the courthouse. There they stand, comrades all, invested with the authority of the community, with helmets, with sticks, with guns, with cattle prods. Facing them are unarmed black people—or, more precisely, they are faced by a group of unarmed people arbitrarily called black, whose color really ranges from the Russian steppes to the Golden Horn, to Zanzibar. In a moment, because he can resolve the situation in no other way, this sheriff, this deputy, this honored American citizen, must begin to club these people down. Some of these people may be related to him by blood; they are assuredly related to the black Mammy of his memory, and the black playmates of his childhood. And for a moment, therefore, he seems nearly to be pleading with the people facing him not to force him to commit yet another crime and not to make yet deeper that ocean of blood in which his conscience is drenched, in which his manhood is perishing. The people do not go away, of course; once a people arise, they never go away, a fact which should be included in the Marine handbook; and the club rises, the blood comes down, and our crimes and our bitterness and our anguish are compounded. Or, one sees it in the eyes of rookie cops in Harlem, who are really among the most terrified people in the world, and who must pretend to themselves that the black mother, the black junkie, the black father, the black child are of a different human species than themselves. They can only deal with their lives and their duties by hiding behind the color curtain. This curtain, indeed, eventually becomes their principal justification for the lives they lead.

But it is not only on this level that one sees the extent of our disaster. Not so very long ago, I found myself in Montgomery, with many, many thousands, marching to the Capitol. Much has been written about this march—for example, the Confederate flag was flying from the Capitol dome; the Federalized National Guard, assigned to protect the marchers, wore Confederate flags on their jackets; if the late Mrs. Viola Liuzzo was avoiding the patrols on that deadly stretch of road that night, she had far sharper eyesight than mine, for I did not see any. Well, there we were, marching to that mansion from which authority had fled. All along that road—I pray that my countrymen will hear me—old, black men and women, who have endured an unspeakable oppression for so long, waved and cheered and sang and wept. They could not march, but they had done something else: they had brought us to the place where we could march. How many of us, after all, were brought up on the white folks leavings, and how mighty a price those old men and women paid to bring those leavings home to us!

We reached the white section of town. There the business-men stood, on balconies, jeering; there stood their maids, in back doors, silent, not daring to wave, but nodding. I watched a black, or rather, a beige-colored woman, standing in the street, watching us thoughtfully; she looked as though she probably held a clerical job in one of those buildings; proof, no doubt, to the jeering white businessmen that the South was making progress. This woman decided to join us, for when we reached the Capitol, I noticed that she was there. But, while we were still marching, through the white part of town, the watching, the waiting, the frightened part of town, we lifted our small American flags, and we faced those eyes—which could not face ours—and we sang. I was next to Harry Belafonte. From upstairs office windows, white Ameri-can secretaries were leaning out of windows, jeering and mocking, and using the ancient Roman sentence of death: thumbs down. Then they saw Harry, who is my very dear friend and a beautiful cat, and who is also, in this most desperately schizophrenic of republics, a major, a reigning matinée idol. One does not need to be a student of Freud to understand what buried forces create a matinée idol, or what he represents to that public which batters down doors to watch him (one need only watch the rise and fall of Ameri-can politicians. This is a sinister observation. And I mean it very seriously). The secretaries were legally white—it was on that basis that they lived their lives, from this principle that they took, collectively, their values; which is, as I have tried to indicate, an interesting spiritual condition. But they were also young. In that ghastly town, they were certainly lonely. They could only, after all, look forward to an alliance, by and by, with one of the jeering businessmen; their boyfriends could only look forward to becoming one of them. And they were also female, a word, which, in the context of the color curtain, has suffered the same fate as the word, "male": it has become practically obscene. When the girls saw Harry Belafonte, a collision occurred in them so visible as to be at once hilarious and unutterably sad. At one moment, the thumbs were down, they were barricaded within their skins, at the next moment, those downturned thumbs flew to their mouths, their fingers pointed, their faces changed, and exactly like bobbysoxers, they oohed, and aahed and moaned. God knows what was happening in the minds and hearts of those girls. Perhaps they would like to be free.

The white man's guilt, which he pretends is due to the fact that the world is a place of many colors, has nothing to do with color. If one attempts to reduce his dilemma to its essence, it really does not have much to do with his crimes, except in the sense that he has locked himself into a place where he is doomed to continue repeating them. The great, unadmitted crime is what he has done to himself. A man is a man, a woman is a woman, and a child is a child. To deny these facts is to open the doors on a chaos deeper and deadlier, and, within the space of a man's lifetime, more timeless, more eternal, than the medieval vision of Hell. And we have arrived at this unspeakable blasphemy in order to acquire things, in order to make money. We cannot endure the things we acquire—the only reason we continually acquire them, like junkies on a hundred dollar a day habit—and our money exists mainly on paper. God help us on that day when the population demands to know what is behind the paper. But, beyond all this, it is terrifying to consider the precise nature of the things we buy with the flesh we sell.

In Henry James' novel *The Ambassadors* published not long before World War I, and not long before his death, he recounts the story of a middle-aged New Englander, assigned by his middle-aged bride-to-be—a widow—the task of rescuing from the flesh-pots of Paris her only son. She wants him to come home to take over the direction of the family factory. In the event, it is the middle-aged New Englander—*The Ambassador*—who is seduced, not so much by Paris, as by a new and less utilitarian view of life. He counsels the young man to "live. Live all you can. It is a mistake not to." Which I translate as meaning "Trust life, and it will teach you, in joy and sorrow, all you need to know." Jazz musicians know this. Those old men and women who waved and sang and wept as we marched in Montgomery know this. White Americans, in the main, do not know this. They are still trapped in that factory to which, in Henry James' novel, the son returns. We never know what this factory produces, for James never tells us. He only conveys to us that the factory, at an unbelievable human expense, produces unnameable objects.

29.722